OpenJS Node.js Application Developer (JSNAD) Certification Guide

A complete practical study guide to become a node.js certified developer with 100+ sample programs demonstrated

Liora Venith

Published by: GitforGits

Publisher: Sonal Dhandre

www.gitforgits.com

support@gitforgits.com

Printed in India

First Printing: October 2024

ISBN: 978-81-19177-95-0

Cover Design by: Kitten Publishing

Prologue

When I first decided to pursue the JSNAD certification, I was thrilled and a little daunted by the incredible scope of knowledge it would bring me. I was excited to dive into the world of asynchronous programming and middleware integration, as well as the challenge of deploying applications and optimizing performance. I knew I needed a structured approach that would not only cover the theoretical aspects but also provide practical insights to help me tackle the exam with confidence. That's why I've crafted this book—to bridge that gap! I dove deep into the core concepts of Node.js, making sure that each chapter built upon the previous one. This created a cohesive and comprehensive learning experience that I'm really excited to share with you! The good news is that I'm going to share the very strategies that helped me navigate complex topics, the resources that were absolutely invaluable during my preparation, and the common pitfalls to avoid. I wanted to create a roadmap that would guide aspiring developers through their certification journey with clarity and assurance.

I've packed this book with all the details you need to know, plus real-world examples and practical exercises to help you really understand the concepts. I've made sure you have all the tools you need to revise quickly and understand even the trickiest concepts with quick reference guides and a glossary of advanced terms. And that's not all! I've also included sample projects and code repositories that mirror the types of challenges you'll face on the certification exam and in professional development environments. Working through these examples has been an amazing way for me to apply theoretical knowledge in a practical context, and I know you'll feel the same!

The more you dive into "JSNAD Certification Preparation," the more you'll see how engaging the material is! I really encourage you to take the time to work through the exercises, explore the sample projects, and reflect on the strategies discussed. It's a great way to really get the most out of the book! This book is so much more than just a study aid! It's a fantastic companion designed to support you every step of the way toward achieving your certification goals.

I know how hard you're working to get your JSNAD certification. That's why I created this book—to make your journey as smooth and effective as possible!

\- Liora Venith

Content

Preface

Get certified in Node.js application development and take your career to the next level! The JSNAD certification is your ticket to proving your deep understanding and proficiency in Node.js application development. This fantastic book is perfect for anyone aiming to ace the JSNAD exam. The book is packed with essential Node.js concepts, including asynchronous programming, middleware integration, and advanced routing techniques. This is your chance to get to grips with the core aspects of Node.js and build a solid foundation! And there's more! You'll also learn about testing strategies, deployment methodologies, and performance optimization.

This book includes quick reference guides and a glossary of advanced terms, making it easy to revisit key concepts and really cement your understanding. You'll also find lots of practical exercises and knowledge checks throughout the book, which are great for checking your understanding and spotting areas you can improve on. And there's more! You'll also find detailed explanations of complex topics that demystify intricate Node.js functionalities, making them accessible and comprehensible.

And there's more! The book also offers access to sample projects and code repositories, providing hands-on experience that mirrors the scenarios encountered in the certification exam. These projects are the perfect chance for learners to put their new skills into practice, building amazing, robust Node.js applications that can scale to any challenge!

In this book you will learn how to:

- Master Node.js architecture and the event-driven, non-blocking I/O model.
- Master asynchronous programming using callbacks, promises, and async/await.
- Implement a robust middleware solution for efficient request handling in Express.js.
- Write unit tests using Mocha and Chai to ensure your code is reliable.
- Use Jest to test the full range of Node.js applications.
- Set up secure environment variables for different stages of deployment.
- Profile and manage your applications' memory to improve performance.
- Deploy your Node.js applications using PM2 and configure Nginx as a reverse proxy.
- Create CI/CD pipelines with GitHub Actions for automated testing and deployment.

GitforGits

Prerequisites

If you're a seasoned developer looking to formalize your expertise with a certification or a newcomer aiming to establish a strong foundation in Node.js, this book is your ticket to success! It will equip you with the knowledge and confidence you need to soar.

Codes Usage

Are you in need of some helpful code examples to assist you in your programming and documentation? Look no further! Our book offers a wealth of supplemental material, including code examples and exercises.

Not only is this book here to aid you in getting your job done, but you have our permission to use the example code in your programs and documentation. However, please note that if you are reproducing a significant portion of the code, we do require you to contact us for permission.

But don't worry, using several chunks of code from this book in your program or answering a question by citing our book and quoting example code does not require permission. But if you do choose to give credit, an attribution typically includes the title, author, publisher, and ISBN. For example, "OpenJS Node.js Application Developer (JSNAD) Certification Guide by Liora Venith ".

If you are unsure whether your intended use of the code examples falls under fair use or the permissions outlined above, please do not hesitate to reach out to us at support@gitforgits.com.

We are happy to assist and clarify any concerns.

Acknowledgement

I owe a tremendous debt of gratitude to GitforGits, for their unflagging enthusiasm and wise counsel throughout the entire process of writing this book. Their knowledge and careful editing helped make sure the piece was useful for people of all reading levels and comprehension skills. In addition, I'd like to thank everyone involved in the publishing process for their efforts in making this book a reality. Their efforts, from copyediting to advertising, made the project what it is today.

Finally, I'd like to express my gratitude to everyone who has shown me unconditional love and encouragement throughout my life. Their support was crucial to the completion of this book. I appreciate your help with this endeavour and your continued interest in my career.

CHAPTER 1: ADVANCED NODE.JS CONCEPTS

Overview

I'm going to take us on a deep dive into some advanced Node.js concepts that are essential for building efficient and high-performance applications. We'll start by taking a closer look at the ins and outs of the Node.js event loop, which is the core mechanism that makes non-blocking I/O and asynchronous operations possible. It's really important to understand how the event loop works if you want to make your code more efficient and avoid performance issues. We'll take a look at each phase of the event loop, see how it handles callbacks, and learn how to use this knowledge to write more efficient code. We'll also look at how to use asynchronous programming patterns, including callbacks, promises, and async/await. Once you're familiar with these patterns, you can write cleaner, more maintainable code and handle complex asynchronous flows more effectively.

Next, we'll take a closer look at buffers and binary data handling, which is really important when you're dealing with files, network communication, and cryptography. You'll learn how Node.js handles binary data with buffers, how to read and write binary streams, and how to use buffers for different applications. We'll also show you how to handle errors and debug your code so that your applications are solid and dependable. You'll learn the best ways to handle errors, check out debugging tools like the Node.js debugger, and use logging techniques to make troubleshooting easier.

Finally, we'll talk about how to use timers and intervals to get the best performance. You'll learn how to schedule tasks effectively using **setTimeout**, **setInterval**, and **setImmediate**, in order to optimize task execution and resource utilization. You'll also see how efficient use of timers can improve application responsiveness and performance. By the end of this chapter, you'll have a solid understanding of these advanced concepts, which will help you develop more efficient and scalable Node.js applications. This foundation will also prepare you for the challenges presented in the JSNAD certification exam.

Intricacies of Node.js Event Loop

If you want to get to grips with the more advanced concepts in Node.js, it's really important to understand the event loop. This is the core mechanism that enables Node.js to perform non-blocking, asynchronous operations. We're going to take a closer look at the event loop now, and we'll go through each of its phases and explain how it handles asynchronous tasks.

Phases of Event Loop

The Node.js event loop operates through a series of phases, each designed to handle specific types of callbacks. By cycling through these phases, the event loop manages the execution of callbacks in a structured manner. The primary phases include:

Timers Phase

In this phase, the event loop executes callbacks scheduled by **setTimeout()** and **setInterval()**. If the specified timer has expired, its callback is placed into the execution queue. It is important to note that the timing is approximate, as the actual execution depends on the event loop's workload and system performance.

Pending Callbacks Phase

During this phase, the event loop processes callbacks for some system operations that were deferred. These include errors from TCP or UDP operations, such as a failed DNS lookup. By handling these callbacks here, Node.js ensures that system-level events are appropriately managed.

Idle, Prepare Phase

This phase is for internal use within Node.js. It allows the system to perform preparatory work before entering the polling phase. Developers typically do not interact directly with this phase, but it is crucial for the smooth operation of the event loop.

Poll Phase

In the poll phase, the event loop retrieves new I/O events and executes callbacks related to I/O operations, excluding timers and **setImmediate()** callbacks. If there are callbacks in the queue, it will process them synchronously until the queue is exhausted or a system-defined limit is reached. If the queue is empty, and there are no timers scheduled, the event loop may block here, waiting for new I/O events.

Check Phase

The check phase handles callbacks scheduled by **setImmediate()**. After the poll phase completes, the event loop will execute all **setImmediate()** callbacks before proceeding. This mechanism provides a way to execute code immediately after the poll phase.

Close Callbacks Phase

In this final phase, the event loop processes close events, such as when a socket or handle is closed abruptly. Callbacks like **socket.on('close', ...)** are executed here, allowing developers to clean up resources and handle disconnections properly.

These above phases allow the event loop to handle asynchronous tasks effectively. When a task needs to be done in the background, Node.js sends it to the system kernel or a worker thread. While the task is running, the event loop continues to do other things. Once the task is finished, its callback is added to a list, and the event loop will run it when it reaches that point.

Event Loop Benefits and Applications

The thing about Node.js is that it's great for all sorts of real-world apps because it can handle asynchronous operations without blocking. If you know how the event loop works, you can build high-performance apps that scale well as below:

High-throughput Web Servers

Web servers built with Node.js can handle thousands of concurrent connections with minimal resource consumption. By using non-blocking I/O and the event loop, the server can process incoming requests asynchronously, initiating database queries or file reads without waiting for them to complete before handling the next request. Companies like Netflix and Walmart have leveraged Node.js to create scalable web services that deliver content to millions of users efficiently.

Real-time Communication Platforms

Applications requiring real-time data transmission, such as chat applications, live collaboration tools, and online gaming platforms, benefit significantly from Node.js's event-driven architecture. By maintaining persistent connections through WebSockets or similar protocols, the event loop can handle incoming and outgoing messages seamlessly. For example, Slack utilizes Node.js to manage real-time messaging and maintain a responsive user experience.

Streaming Data Applications

Node.js excels in applications that involve streaming data, such as media streaming services or data processing pipelines. By using streams and the event loop, these applications can handle large amounts of data incrementally, reducing memory usage and improving performance. Companies like Netflix use Node.js to build streaming services that deliver content smoothly to users worldwide.

Microservices Architecture

In a microservices architecture, applications are decomposed into smaller, independently deployable services. Node.js's lightweight nature and efficient event loop make it an excellent choice for building microservices that need to handle high volumes of network requests. By managing asynchronous communication between services effectively, Node.js enables organizations like PayPal to scale their systems and improve deployment agility.

IoT Systems

IoT applications often involve handling data from numerous sensors and devices simultaneously. Node.js, with its event loop, can manage multiple concurrent I/O operations, making it suitable for IoT systems that require real-time data processing and control. For instance, Microsoft Azure's IoT services use Node.js to process data from millions of devices, enabling real-time analytics and responsive actions.

API Gateways and Proxies

API gateways and proxies act as intermediaries between clients and backend services, handling tasks like authentication, rate limiting, and data aggregation. Node.js's ability to handle numerous concurrent connections and manage asynchronous I/O makes it ideal for building efficient API gateways. Companies like Express and Koa provide frameworks that simplify the creation of such services, leveraging the event loop for high performance.

This knowledge is crucial for building applications that are not only high-performing but also scalable and resilient. Real-world applications across various industries showcase the event loop's power in handling concurrent connections, processing real-time data, and enabling responsive user experiences.

Asynchronous Programming Patterns

Think about a book publishing platform that works like an e-commerce website. This platform lets users browse books, place orders, write reviews, and authors upload new manuscripts. To make sure everything runs smoothly for users, you've got to be good at asynchronous programming.

If you want to manage asynchronous operations in Node.js effectively, you need to understand advanced patterns like callbacks, promises, and async/await. These patterns let developers handle operations like database queries, file uploads, and network requests without blocking the event loop.

Callbacks

At the core of asynchronous programming in Node.js are callbacks. A callback is a function passed as an argument to another function, executed after the completion of an operation. In our book publishing platform, when a user places an order, the application might need to:

- Validate the user's payment information.
- Update the inventory.
- Send a confirmation email.

By using callbacks, each of these operations can be executed asynchronously as shown below:

```
function placeOrder(orderDetails, callback) {

  processPayment(orderDetails, function(paymentErr,
paymentResult) {

    if (paymentErr) return callback(paymentErr);

    updateInventory(orderDetails, function(inventoryErr,
inventoryResult) {
```

```
      if (inventoryErr) return callback(inventoryErr);
      sendConfirmationEmail(orderDetails, function(emailErr,
emailResult) {
        if (emailErr) return callback(emailErr);
        callback(null, 'Order placed successfully');
      });
    });
  });
}
```

However, callbacks can lead to deeply nested code, often referred to as "callback hell," making it difficult to read and maintain.

Promises

To address the drawbacks of callbacks, promises provide a cleaner way to handle asynchronous operations by allowing chaining and better error handling. A promise represents a value that may be available now, in the future, or never. By rewriting the previous example using promises:

```
function placeOrder(orderDetails) {
  return processPayment(orderDetails)
    .then(paymentResult => updateInventory(orderDetails))
    .then(inventoryResult =>
sendConfirmationEmail(orderDetails))
    .then(emailResult => 'Order placed successfully')
    .catch(error => {
      throw error;
    });
}
```

Promises help flatten the code structure and make the flow of asynchronous operations more manageable. In our platform, this approach simplifies handling multiple asynchronous tasks that depend on each other.

Async/Await

Async/await is syntactic sugar built on top of promises, introduced in ECMAScript 2017. It allows writing asynchronous code that looks synchronous, improving readability. By using **async** functions and the **await** keyword, developers can write code that is easier to understand and maintain.

Using async/await, the **placeOrder** function becomes:

```
async function placeOrder(orderDetails) {
  try {
    await processPayment(orderDetails);
    await updateInventory(orderDetails);
    await sendConfirmationEmail(orderDetails);
    return 'Order placed successfully';
  } catch (error) {
    throw error;
  }
}
```

This code resembles synchronous code, making it easier to follow the execution flow. In the context of our book publishing platform, async/await simplifies the management of complex asynchronous workflows.

Managing Complex Asynchronous Workflows

In a practical setting like our e-commerce platform, managing multiple operations that may be related and running at the same time is common. For instance, when an author uploads a new manuscript, the platform might need to:

- Store the file in cloud storage.
- Extract metadata (title, author, keywords).
- Generate a preview.
- Notify subscribers about the new release.

Some of these tasks can run concurrently, while others depend on the completion of previous tasks.

Parallel Execution with Promises

To execute tasks in parallel, promises can be used with **Promise.all()**. This method takes an array of promises and returns a single promise that resolves when all the promises in the array have resolved.

```
async function handleNewManuscript(uploadDetails) {
  try {
    const [storageResult, metadata] = await Promise.all([
      storeFile(uploadDetails.file),
      extractMetadata(uploadDetails.file)
    ]);
    await generatePreview(uploadDetails.file);
    await notifySubscribers(metadata);
    return 'Manuscript processed successfully';
  } catch (error) {
    throw error;
  }
}
```

In this example, **storeFile** and **extractMetadata** run concurrently, optimizing the processing time. Once both are completed, the application proceeds to generate a preview and notify subscribers.

Sequential Execution with Async/Await

When tasks need to be executed in a specific order, async/await ensures that each operation waits for the previous one to complete before proceeding.

```
async function processOrder(orderDetails) {
  try {
    const paymentResult = await processPayment(orderDetails);
    const inventoryResult = await
updateInventory(orderDetails);
    const emailResult = await
sendConfirmationEmail(orderDetails);
    return 'Order processed successfully';
  } catch (error) {
    throw error;
```

```
  }
}
```

This sequential execution ensures that the inventory is only updated after the payment is successful, and the confirmation email is sent after the inventory update.

Handling Multiple Independent Operations

Sometimes, the application needs to perform multiple independent asynchronous operations and proceed once all have completed. For instance, when generating the homepage, the platform might need to fetch:

- Featured books.
- Latest reviews.
- Top authors.

By using **Promise.all()**, these can be fetched concurrently:

```
async function loadHomePage() {
  try {
    const [featuredBooks, latestReviews, topAuthors] = await
Promise.all([
      getFeaturedBooks(),
      getLatestReviews(),
      getTopAuthors()
    ]);
    return renderHomePage({ featuredBooks, latestReviews,
topAuthors });
  } catch (error) {
    console.error('Error loading home page:', error);
    throw error;
  }
}
```

This approach shaves off some of the loading time, which is good for the user experience.

Cancellation and Timeouts

In certain scenarios, it may be necessary to cancel asynchronous operations or enforce timeouts. While promises do not natively support cancellation, developers can implement custom logic or use libraries that provide this functionality.

```
async function fetchWithTimeout(url, timeout) {
  const controller = new AbortController();
  const id = setTimeout(() => controller.abort(), timeout);
  try {
    const response = await fetch(url, { signal: 
controller.signal });
    clearTimeout(id);
    return response;
  } catch (error) {
    console.error('Fetch aborted:', error);
    throw error;
  }
}
```

Now this, in our platform, could be used to prevent long-running requests from affecting application performance.

Deep Dive into Buffers and Binary Data Handling

Node.js is all about buffers. They're key for working with binary data, helping us process files, network packets, and other binary streams more effectively. Buffers let us work directly with raw binary data, which is key for tasks that need high performance and precise data manipulation on our book publishing platform.

Understanding Buffers

A buffer is a fixed-length sequence of bytes. Unlike standard JavaScript strings or arrays, buffers are designed to handle raw binary data, making them ideal for reading and writing files or handling network communications.

```
// Creating a buffer from a string
const buf = Buffer.from('Node.js Buffer Example', 'utf8');
// Allocating a buffer of a specific size (e.g., 256 bytes)
const bufAlloc = Buffer.alloc(256);
```

Buffers can be created from strings, arrays, or by allocating a specific amount of memory. They support various encoding formats like UTF-8, ASCII, and binary.

Reading and Writing Binary Data

In our e-commerce platform, handling book cover images, PDF files, or user-uploaded content requires reading and writing binary data. Using buffers, we can read files into memory and process them as needed.

- Reading a file into a buffer:

```
const fs = require('fs');
// Reading a binary file asynchronously
fs.readFile('book-cover.jpg', (err, data) => {
  if (err) throw err;
  // 'data' is a buffer containing the binary file data
  console.log('File size:', data.length);
});
```

- Writing a buffer to a file:

```
const fs = require('fs');
// Writing binary data to a file
const buf = Buffer.from([0x42, 0x4F, 0x4F, 0x4B]); //
Represents 'BOOK' in ASCII
fs.writeFile('output.bin', buf, (err) => {
  if (err) throw err;
  console.log('Binary data written successfully');
});
```

You can manipulate the binary data directly by reading files into buffers. This lets you do things like resize images, encrypt files, or modify content before saving.

Manipulating Binary Streams

When you're working with streams, buffers are a must-have. They let you handle large amounts of data quickly and efficiently, and they don't load everything into memory. Let's say a user uploads a large manuscript:

```
const http = require('http');
const fs = require('fs');
http.createServer((req, res) => {
  if (req.method === 'POST' && req.url === '/upload') {
    const fileStream =
fs.createWriteStream('uploads/manuscript.pdf');
    req.pipe(fileStream);
    req.on('end', () => {
      res.end('Upload complete');
    });
    req.on('error', (err) => {
      console.error('Error during upload:', err);
      res.statusCode = 500;
      res.end('Server error');
    });
  }
}).listen(8080);
```

In this case, the data from the HTTP request is sent straight to a file that can be modified. Buffers process chunks of data, so large files don't use all your system memory.

Network Communication with Buffers

The thing about network protocols and real-time data transmission is that buffers let us send and receive binary data over sockets.

```
const net = require('net');
// Server
```

```
const server = net.createServer((socket) => {
  socket.on('data', (data) => {
    // 'data' is a buffer
    console.log('Received:', data.toString('utf8'));
    // Sending a response
    const response = Buffer.from('Acknowledged', 'utf8');
    socket.write(response);
  });
});
server.listen(5000, () => {
  console.log('Server listening on port 5000');
});
// Client
const client = net.createConnection({ port: 5000 }, () => {
  const message = Buffer.from('Hello Server', 'utf8');
  client.write(message);
});
client.on('data', (data) => {
  console.log('Server response:', data.toString('utf8'));
  client.end();
});
```

In our platform, this would facilitate real-time notifications, chat features between authors and editors, or live updates on book availability.

Working with Binary Protocols

Buffer zones help us to parse and construct binary communication protocols. For instance, if the platform is hooked up to an old system that uses a binary protocol, we can use buffers to encode and decode messages.

```
// Assuming a message format where the first byte is a
command, followed by data
```

```
function parseMessage(buffer) {
  const command = buffer.readUInt8(0);
  const data = buffer.slice(1);
  switch (command) {
    case 0x01:
      console.log('Command: Login');
      // Process login data
      break;
    case 0x02:
      console.log('Command: Upload');
      // Process upload data
      break;
    default:
      console.log('Unknown command');
  }
}
```

Buffer Encoding and Decoding

Buffers support various encodings, which is useful when converting between different data formats.

```
const buf = Buffer.from('Sample Text', 'utf8');
// Converting to Base64
const base64Str = buf.toString('base64');
console.log('Base64 Encoded:', base64Str);
// Converting back to UTF-8
const utf8Str = Buffer.from(base64Str,
'base64').toString('utf8');
console.log('UTF-8 Decoded:', utf8Str);
```

This feature is great for converting binary data to text for transfer via text-only protocols like

HTTP headers or JSON payloads. In our e-commerce book publishing platform, using buffers helps us process large files more quickly, improve data transmission, and provide a solid experience for users engaging with rich media content.

Effective Error Handling

Our e-commerce book publishing platform has to be able to handle errors without any hiccups so that users have a smooth experience and the system stays stable. This is where we'll look at ways to handle errors and debug issues, identify scenarios that need attention, and show you how to implement solutions.

In complex applications, errors can arise from various sources:

- **Unhandled Exceptions**: When the application encounters unexpected input or conditions not accounted for in the code.
- **Asynchronous Errors**: Mistakes in handling asynchronous operations leading to callbacks or promises not resolving as intended.
- **Resource Leaks**: Improper management of resources like database connections or file handles causing memory leaks.
- **Performance Bottlenecks**: Slow response times due to inefficient code or blocking operations.
- **Logical Errors**: Flaws in business logic resulting in incorrect behavior, such as miscalculations in order totals.

The way it works on our platform is that if a user tries to place an order but the payment can't go through because of an unhandled exception in the payment module, we'll know about it.

Using 'Try/Catch' Blocks

If you put code that might throw exceptions into a try/catch block, it'll let the app deal with errors in a nice, smooth way.

```
async function processPayment(orderDetails) {
  try {
    // Code that may throw an error
    const paymentResult = await
paymentGateway.charge(orderDetails);
    return paymentResult;
  } catch (error) {
    // Handle specific errors
```

```
    if (error.code === 'INSUFFICIENT_FUNDS') {
      throw new Error('Payment declined due to insufficient
funds');
    } else {
      // Log and rethrow for upstream handling
      console.error('Payment processing error:', error);
      throw error;
    }
  }
}
```

This example shows how to identify and handle specific errors in a way that gives the user helpful feedback.

Propagating Errors

If you make sure that errors are passed on from one function to the next, it gives the higher-level functions the option to handle them however they need to.

```
async function placeOrder(orderDetails) {
  try {
    await processPayment(orderDetails);
    await updateInventory(orderDetails);
    await sendConfirmationEmail(orderDetails);
    return 'Order placed successfully';
  } catch (error) {
    // Centralized error handling
    console.error('Error placing order:', error);
    throw error; // Propagate error to the API response layer
  }
}
```

Here, by rethrowing errors, the application can maintain a centralized error handling strategy.

Using Promises with Error Handling

If you're working with promises, it's a good idea to attach a .catch() handler so you can catch any errors.

```
function sendConfirmationEmail(orderDetails) {
  return emailService.send(orderDetails)
    .catch(error => {
      console.error('Email sending failed:', error);
      throw new Error('Failed to send confirmation email');
    });
}
```

This approach prevents unhandled promise rejections, which can cause the application to crash.

Creating Custom Error Classes

It's helpful to define custom error classes so we can provide more context and handle errors more precisely.

```
class PaymentError extends Error {
  constructor(message, code) {
    super(message);
    this.name = 'PaymentError';
    this.code = code;
  }
}
// Usage
throw new PaymentError('Payment declined',
'PAYMENT_DECLINED');
```

Here, in the error handling middleware, the application can check the error type and respond accordingly.

Implementing Error Handling Middleware

In tools like Express, error handling middleware can spot mistakes and format responses.

```
// Error handling middleware
app.use((err, req, res, next) => {
  console.error('Unhandled error:', err);
  res.status(500).json({ message: 'An unexpected error
occurred' });
});
```

This ensures that users receive consistent error messages and that sensitive error details are not exposed.

Debugging Techniques

When errors occur, debugging helps identify and resolve the underlying issues. Effective debugging strategies include:

Using Node.js Debugger

The Node.js debugger allows stepping through code to inspect variables and execution flow.

```
First, run the application with the --inspect flag.
node --inspect app.js
```

Then, open chrome://inspect in Chrome to connect to the debugger.

```
Then, use the debugger statement in code.
function processOrder(orderDetails) {
  debugger; // Execution will pause here
  // Rest of the code
}
```

In our platform, this helps identify where the order processing is failing.

Utilizing Console Logging

The thing with adding **console.log()** statements is that they help you understand what's going on with variables and how things are working.

```
function updateInventory(orderDetails) {
```

```
  console.log('Updating inventory for order:',
orderDetails.orderId);
  // Code to update inventory
}
```

While simple, logging is effective for quick debugging but should be used judiciously to avoid cluttering the console.

Employing Advanced Logging Libraries

We can use libraries like winston or bunyan offers more control over logging levels and outputs.

```
const winston = require('winston');
const logger = winston.createLogger({
  level: 'info',
  transports: [
    new winston.transports.Console(),
    new winston.transports.File({ filename: 'application.log'
})
  ]
});
logger.info('Application started');
logger.error('An error occurred:', error);
```

The good thing about structured logging is that it makes it easier to analyze logs and integrate them with monitoring tools.

Inspecting Memory Usage

For issues like memory leaks, tools like **heapdump** can capture snapshots for analysis.

```
const heapdump = require('heapdump');
// Trigger heap dump when needed
heapdump.writeSnapshot('heap-' + Date.now() +
'.heapsnapshot');
```

Here, the snapshot can be analyzed using Chrome DevTools to identify memory leaks.

Using Profiling Tools

Profiling helps detect performance bottlenecks. For example, we can use the **--inspect** flag and Chrome DevTools to record CPU usage. And, also libraries like toobusy-js can monitor event loop delays.

```
const toobusy = require('toobusy-js');
if (toobusy()) {
  // The event loop is lagging
  res.status(503).send('Server is busy');
}
```

In our platform, profiling might reveal that synchronous code is blocking the event loop during peak traffic.

By following these techniques, users can place orders, upload content, and interact with the system without any unexpected errors or performance problems. Following best practices helps us solve current issues and makes it easier to maintain the application long-term.

Utilizing Timers and Intervals for Optimized Performance

The timers in Node.js are great for scheduling tasks and managing asynchronous operations in a smooth and efficient way. Using things like **setTimeout**, **setInterval**, and **setImmediate** lets developers control when code is run, which helps make applications run more smoothly. In our app, making the most of these timers can improve the user experience and help us manage our resources better.

Using 'setTimeout'

The **setTimeout** function is useful for tasks that need to be executed after a certain delay. In our platform, suppose we want to send a reminder email to users who have items in their cart but have not completed the purchase within 24 hours.

```
function scheduleAbandonedCartEmail(userId, cartItems) {
  const delay = 24 * 60 * 60 * 1000; // 24 hours in
milliseconds
```

```
  setTimeout(() => {
    sendAbandonedCartEmail(userId, cartItems);
  }, delay);
}
```

In this example, by scheduling the email after 24 hours, we avoid immediate processing, reducing the load on the email service.

Using 'setInterval'

The **setInterval** function is ideal for tasks that need to run repeatedly at fixed intervals. For instance, we might want to check for new book releases from authors and update the homepage accordingly every hour.

```
function updateHomepageFeaturedBooks() {
  setInterval(async () => {
    const newBooks = await fetchNewReleases();
    displayFeaturedBooks(newBooks);
  }, 60 * 60 * 1000); // Every hour
}
updateHomepageFeaturedBooks();
```

Here's how it works:

- It keeps the homepage content fresh, so users see the latest releases.
- It optimizes the update process without any manual intervention. This makes things consistent.

Using 'setImmediate'

The **setImmediate** function schedules a callback to execute after the current event loop phase. This is useful when you want to defer a task until the current operations complete but without significant delay.

```
function processUserRegistration(userData) {
  saveUserData(userData);
  setImmediate(() => {
    sendWelcomeEmail(userData.email);
```

```
  });
}
processUserRegistration(newUser);
```

In this scenario, we're aiming to:

- Send a welcome email right away after a new user registers.
- Let the main thread finish up some important tasks before sending the email, so we can avoid any blocks.

To sum up, these timers help manage asynchronous operations, maintain responsiveness, and ensure efficient resource utilization.

Summary

In a nutshell, we looked at some of the more advanced concepts in Node.js that are essential for developing high-performance applications. We took a close look at how Node.js manages asynchronous operations through its various phases, exploring the intricacies of the event loop in the process. We took a close look at techniques like callbacks, promises, and async/await, showing how they make it easier to handle asynchronous tasks. With some practical examples involving a book publishing platform, it became clear how these patterns could make complex workflows simpler, make code easier to read, and make it easier to maintain.

We also took a detailed look at buffers and how to handle binary data in Node.js. By using buffers, developers learned how to read, write, and manipulate binary streams, which was key for tasks like file handling and network communication. We also went over some great strategies for handling and debugging errors. We also looked at ways to spot potential problems early on and put in place solid error management. By using tools like try/catch blocks, custom error classes, and the Node.js debugger and logging libraries, developers could make their apps more stable, spot and fix problems faster, and give users a better experience.

Finally, we looked at how to use timers and intervals to make things run more smoothly. We learned about setTimeout, setInterval, and setImmediate, which are useful for scheduling tasks. By using these timers in the right way, developers can make apps run faster, stop them from blocking the event loop, and make the user experience better. The knowledge from this chapter is a great start for tackling more complex challenges in Node.js programming.

Knowledge Exercise

1. Which phase of the Node.js event loop is responsible for executing callbacks scheduled by **setTimeout** and **setInterval**?

A. Poll Phase

B. Timers Phase

C. Check Phase

D. Pending Callbacks Phase

2. In the context of the event loop, what is the primary purpose of the Poll Phase?

A. Executing **setImmediate** callbacks

B. Handling I/O events and executing I/O-related callbacks

C. Processing close event callbacks

D. Executing microtasks like promises

3. What is the main disadvantage of using callbacks for asynchronous operations in Node.js?

A. Increased memory usage

B. Difficulty in handling errors and "callback hell"

C. Incompatibility with Node.js modules

D. Slower execution compared to synchronous code

4. How do promises improve the management of asynchronous operations compared to callbacks?

A. By making code synchronous

B. By allowing chaining and better error handling

C. By reducing code execution time

D. By eliminating the need for error handling

5. Which of the following is a correct way to create a buffer from a string in Node.js?

A. const buf = new Buffer('Sample Text');

B. const buf = Buffer.alloc('Sample Text');

C. const buf = Buffer.from('Sample Text', 'utf8');

D. const buf = Buffer.create('Sample Text');

6. What is the advantage of using buffers when handling file operations in Node.js?

A. Buffers are faster than streams

B. Buffers allow manipulation of raw binary data efficiently

C. Buffers automatically convert data to JSON

D. Buffers simplify handling of large files by loading them entirely into memory

7. Which method would you use to execute a function immediately after the current event loop phase completes?

A. **setTimeout(fn, 0)**

B. **setImmediate(fn)**

C. **process.nextTick(fn)**

D. **setInterval(fn, 0)**

8. In error handling, what is the benefit of creating custom error classes in Node.js applications?

A. They reduce the size of error objects

B. They allow for more precise error identification and handling

C. They automatically log errors to external services

D. They prevent the application from throwing exceptions

9. When working with asynchronous functions using async/await, how do you handle errors appropriately?

A. By ignoring errors and letting them fail silently

B. By using try/catch blocks around await expressions

C. By attaching **.then()** and **.catch()** to the async function

D. By converting the function back to a callback

10. What is the primary difference between **setImmediate** and **process.nextTick** in Node.js?

A. **setImmediate** executes callbacks before I/O events, **process.nextTick** after

B. **setImmediate** is deprecated, **process.nextTick** is the standard

C. **process.nextTick** executes callbacks before the next event loop tick, **setImmediate** after

D. They are functionally identical and can be used interchangeably

11. Which of the following statements about the event loop is true?

A. It blocks during synchronous operations

B. It can handle only one I/O operation at a time

C. It allows Node.js to perform non-blocking I/O operations

D. It replaces the need for multithreading in all cases

12. In the context of our book publishing platform, why might you use **Promise.all()**?

A. To execute multiple asynchronous tasks sequentially

B. To execute multiple asynchronous tasks in parallel and wait for all to complete

C. To handle errors from multiple promises individually

D. To cancel all promises if one fails

13. How does using **async/await** improve code readability in asynchronous operations?

A. By making asynchronous code appear synchronous

B. By removing the need for error handling

C. By eliminating the use of promises

D. By enforcing strict typing

14. What is a common cause of "callback hell" in Node.js applications?

A. Overusing synchronous functions

B. Nesting multiple callbacks within each other

C. Using too many third-party modules

D. Improper error handling in promises

15. When should you use **setInterval** over **setTimeout**?

A. When you need to execute a function once after a delay

B. When you want to defer execution until the event loop is idle

C. When you need to execute a function repeatedly at fixed intervals

D. When you need to execute a function immediately

Answers and Explanations

1. B. Timers Phase

The Timers Phase is responsible for executing callbacks scheduled by **setTimeout** and **setInterval**. It checks if any timers have expired and runs their callbacks accordingly.

2. B. Handling I/O events and executing I/O-related callbacks

The Poll Phase retrieves new I/O events and executes their callbacks. It processes events like network requests and file system operations.

3. B. Difficulty in handling errors and "callback hell"

Callbacks can lead to deeply nested code structures, making it hard to read and maintain. This situation is often referred to as "callback hell."

4. B. By allowing chaining and better error handling

Promises improve asynchronous code management by enabling chaining of asynchronous operations and providing a more straightforward way to handle errors through **.then()** and **.catch()** methods.

5. C. **const buf = Buffer.from('Sample Text', 'utf8');**

The **Buffer.from()** method creates a new buffer from a string, with the specified encoding (UTF-8 in this case).

6. B. Buffers allow manipulation of raw binary data efficiently

Buffers are designed to handle raw binary data, making them ideal for reading and writing files or handling binary streams without the overhead of character encoding conversions.

7. B. **setImmediate(fn)**

The **setImmediate()** function schedules a callback to execute immediately after the current event loop phase completes.

8. B. They allow for more precise error identification and handling

Custom error classes enable developers to create specific error types, making it easier to identify and handle different error conditions appropriately.

9. B. By using try/catch blocks around await expressions

When using async/await, errors can be caught using try/catch blocks, allowing for proper error handling in asynchronous functions.

10. C. **process.nextTick** executes callbacks before the next event loop tick, **setImmediate** after

process.nextTick() schedules a callback to execute before the event loop continues, giving it higher priority, while **setImmediate()** executes after the current poll phase.

11. C. It allows Node.js to perform non-blocking I/O operations

The event loop enables Node.js to handle asynchronous operations without blocking, allowing for efficient processing of multiple I/O operations concurrently.

12. B. To execute multiple asynchronous tasks in parallel and wait for all to complete

Promise.all() runs multiple promises in parallel and resolves when all of them have completed, which is useful for tasks like fetching data from multiple sources simultaneously.

13. A. By making asynchronous code appear synchronous

Async/await syntax allows developers to write asynchronous code that looks and behaves like synchronous code, improving readability and maintainability.

14. B. Nesting multiple callbacks within each other

"Callback hell" occurs when callbacks are nested within other callbacks multiple levels deep, leading to hard-to-read and hard-to-maintain code.

15. C. When you need to execute a function repeatedly at fixed intervals

setInterval is used for scheduling a function to run repeatedly at specified intervals, whereas **setTimeout** schedules a one-time execution after a delay.

CHAPTER 2: MODULE SYSTEMS AND PACKAGE MANAGEMENT

Overview

In this chapter, we'll dive deep into the advanced aspects of Node.js module systems and package management. We begin by examining advanced methods for utilizing Node.js modules, improving our approach to code structuring and organization. You will master these techniques and create maintainable and scalable applications that adhere to best practices essential for complex development and the JSNAD certification. Furthermore, we analyze how modules interact within an application and optimize their usage to achieve superior performance.

Next, we'll create and manage NPM packages. This section will show you how to publish your own packages, handle dependencies effectively, and follow best practices. We also cover versioning and compatibility, which are crucial for professional development and maintaining reliable applications. We then move on to monorepos and workspace management, examining how to handle multiple packages within a single repository. By understanding monorepos, we can efficiently manage large codebases and simplify dependencies across projects. This knowledge helps us maintain code quality and reduce duplication.

Finally, we delve into leveraging native modules for enhanced functionality and discuss dependency injection and modular design patterns. These topics equip us to build robust applications with clean, testable codebases.

Advanced Techniques with Node.js Modules

I'm going to tell you why mastering module systems is vital for modern Node.js development. It's because you need to build scalable and maintainable applications. Node.js provides two main module systems: CommonJS and ES6 modules. If you understand how to use these systems effectively, you can organize your codebases efficiently, which means better collaboration and code reuse. In our book publishing platform, we've seen first-hand how leveraging these module systems enhances the application's structure and facilitates growth.

CommonJS Modules

CommonJS is the original module system used in Node.js. It uses the **require()** function to import modules and the **module.exports** or **exports** object to export them. This system loads modules synchronously, making it straightforward and easy to use.

Following is an example of a CommonJS module:

```
// file: utils/logger.js
function logInfo(message) {
  console.log(`[INFO]: ${message}`);
}
```

```
function logError(error) {
  console.error(`[ERROR]: ${error}`);
}
module.exports = {
  logInfo,
  logError,
};

// file: app.js
const logger = require('./utils/logger');
logger.logInfo('Application started');
```

The best way to make the codebase more manageable is to use CommonJS modules. These divide functionalities into separate files. By exporting specific functions or objects, we ensure that only the necessary components are accessible to other parts of the application.

ES6 Modules

ES6 modules, introduced in ECMAScript 2015, provide a standardized module system. They use **import** and **export** statements, allowing both named and default exports. Unlike CommonJS, ES6 modules can be loaded asynchronously, which can improve performance.

Following is an example of an ES6 module:

```
// file: services/userService.mjs
export function createUser(userData) {
  // Logic to create a new user
}
export function getUserById(userId) {
  // Logic to retrieve a user by ID
}



// file: app.mjs
```

```
import { createUser, getUserById } from
'./services/userService.mjs';

createUser({ name: 'Alice', email: 'alice@example.com' });
```

Now, to use ES6 modules in Node.js, we need to set **"type": "module"** in the **package.json** file or use the **.mjs** file extension. This informs Node.js to interpret files as ES6 modules.

Organizing Codebase with Modules

The application should be structured using modules, separating concerns and improving maintainability. Our book publishing platform will be organised into modules such as:

- **`models/`**: Database models for users, books, orders.
- **`controllers/`**: Handling HTTP requests and responses.
- **`services/`**: Business logic and operations.
- **`utils/`**: Utility functions and helpers.
- **`routes/`**: API route definitions.

Following is the directory structure:

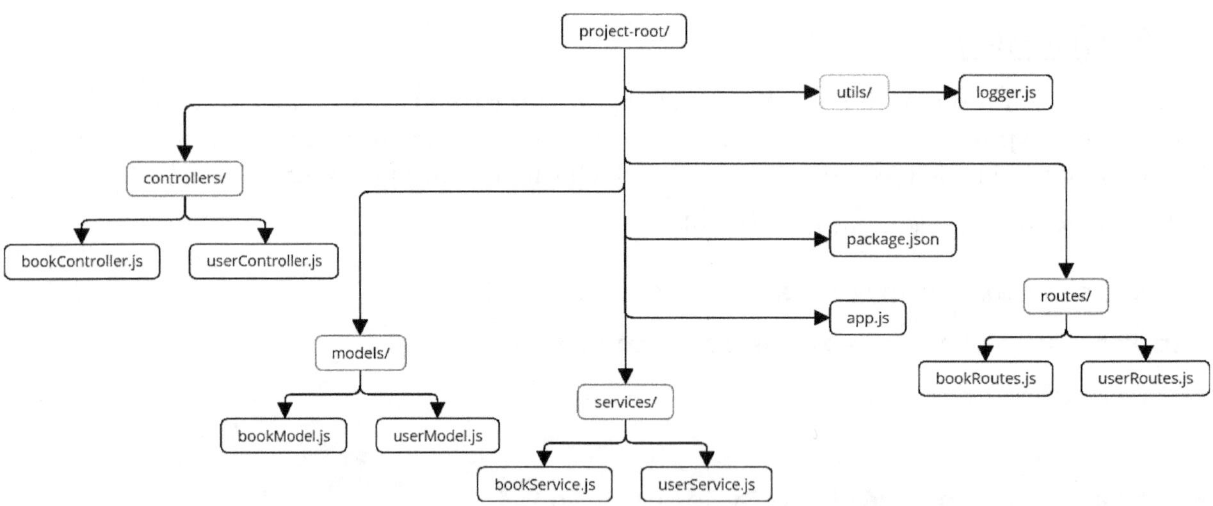

Fig 2.1 Directory Structure

Implementing Modules in Platform

Consider the example of a Book Service Module:

```
// file: services/bookService.js
const Book = require('../models/bookModel');
function addNewBook(bookData) {
  const book = new Book(bookData);
  return book.save();
}
function getAllBooks() {
  return Book.find();
}
module.exports = {
  addNewBook,
  getAllBooks,
};
```

Now let us use the Book Service in a Controller:

```
// file: controllers/bookController.js
const { addNewBook, getAllBooks } =
require('../services/bookService');
function createBook(req, res) {
  addNewBook(req.body)
    .then((book) => res.status(201).json(book))
    .catch((error) => res.status(500).json({ error:
error.message }));
}
function listBooks(req, res) {
  getAllBooks()
    .then((books) => res.json(books))
    .catch((error) => res.status(500).json({ error:
error.message }));
}
```

```
module.exports = {
  createBook,
  listBooks,
};
```

By separating the business logic into services and keeping controllers focused on handling requests and responses, we achieve a clean separation of concerns. This modularity simplifies testing and future modifications.

Scalability through Modularity

As the platform grows, adding new features or modifying existing ones becomes more manageable. For instance, if we need to implement a new payment gateway, we can create a separate module without affecting other parts of the application.

- Creating a Payment Module:

```
// file: services/paymentService.js
function processPayment(paymentDetails) {
  // Logic to process payment with a gateway
}
module.exports = {
  processPayment,
};
```

- Integrating the Payment Module:

```
// file: controllers/orderController.js
const { processPayment } =
require('../services/paymentService');
function placeOrder(req, res) {
  processPayment(req.body.paymentDetails)
    .then(() => {
      // Logic to save order
      res.status(201).json({ message: 'Order placed
successfully' });
```

```
    })
    .catch((error) => res.status(500).json({ error:
error.message }));
}
module.exports = {
  placeOrder,
};
```

We can easily replace or update the payment gateway without significant changes to other modules by modularizing the payment logic.

Maintainability with Clear Module Boundaries

It is absolutely essential to define clear interfaces between modules. This ensures that changes within a module have minimal impact on others. Let me give you an example. If we decide to change the database from MongoDB to PostgreSQL, we only need to update the models and services interacting with the database.

The following will show you how to abstract database operations.

```
// file: models/db.js
let dbClient;
function connect(connectionString) {
  // Logic to connect to the database
  dbClient = /* ... */;
}
function getClient() {
  return dbClient;
}
module.exports = {
  connect,
  getClient,
};
```

By using an abstraction layer, other modules interact with the database through a consistent interface, making the underlying implementation interchangeable.

ES6 Modules for Tooling

ES6 modules also provides better static analysis and tooling support due to their standardized syntax. Tools like ESLint and TypeScript can analyze imports and exports more effectively, catching errors at compile time.

Let us try converting to ES6 Modules:

```
// file: controllers/bookController.mjs
import { addNewBook, getAllBooks } from
'../services/bookService.mjs';
export function createBook(req, res) {
  // Same as before
}
export function listBooks(req, res) {
  // Same as before
}
```

Mixing CommonJS and ES6 Modules

In some cases, we will use both module systems, especially when working with third-party libraries that use CommonJS. The Node.js framework allows for seamless interoperability between the two systems, despite a few minor limitations.

I'm going to show you how to import a CommonJS module in ES6.

```
// file: app.mjs
import express from 'express';
import logger from './utils/logger.js'; // Assuming logger.js
uses CommonJS
const app = express();
app.listen(3000, () => {
  logger.logInfo('Server started on port 3000');
});
```

In this example, we can import CommonJS modules into an ES6 module using default imports.

However, named exports from CommonJS modules may require additional handling.

Index Files for Simplified Imports

To simplify import statements, we can use index files that re-export modules from a directory.

Following is an example of an Index File:

```
// file: services/index.js
module.exports = {
  userService: require('./userService'),
  bookService: require('./bookService'),
  paymentService: require('./paymentService'),
};
```

Below is the use of the Index File:

```
// file: controllers/orderController.js
const { paymentService } = require('../services');
function placeOrder(req, res) {
  paymentService.processPayment(req.body.paymentDetails)
    .then(() => {
      // Logic to save order
      res.status(201).json({ message: 'Order placed
successfully' });
    })
    .catch((error) => res.status(500).json({ error:
error.message }));
}
```

By aggregating exports, we reduce the complexity of import statements, making the code cleaner.

Creating and Managing NPM Packages

In the Node.js ecosystem, creating and managing NPM (Node Package Manager) packages is a fundamental skill that every developer should have. It empowers them to share code, reuse functionalities, and contribute to the community. Our book publishing platform will have functionalities that are common across different services, such as formatting book titles, calculating royalties, or handling authentication. The best way to achieve better code reuse and consistency is to package these functionalities.

Initializing a New NPM Package

To begin creating an NPM package, we start by setting up a new project directory and initializing it.

Create a New Directory

Navigate to your workspace and create a new directory for the package.

```
mkdir book-utils
cd book-utils
```

Initialize the Package

Use **npm init** to create a **package.json** file, which contains metadata about the package.

```
npm init
```

Follow the prompts to provide details such as package name, version, description, entry point, test command, repository URL, keywords, author, and license.

Developing Package Functionality

Suppose we want to create a utility package that provides common book-related functions.

Create the Main Module File

In the package directory, create an **index.js** file that will serve as the entry point.

```
// file: index.js
function formatTitle(title) {
  return title.trim().replace(/\s+/g, ' ').toUpperCase();
}
function calculateRoyalties(sales, rate) {
  return sales * rate;
}
```

```
module.exports = {
  formatTitle,
  calculateRoyalties,
};
```

Adding Dependencies

If our package relies on external modules, we need to install and manage them.

```
npm install lodash
```

Then, include it in our code:

```
const _ = require('lodash');
function generateSlug(title) {
  return _.kebabCase(title);
}
module.exports = {
  // Previous exports
  generateSlug,
};
```

The **lodash** package will be listed under **dependencies** in **package.json**.

By creating and managing NPM packages effectively, we enhance our ability to build modular, maintainable applications.

Monorepos and Workspace Management

Understanding Monorepositories

In modern application development, managing multiple packages within a single repository—known as a monorepository or monorepo—has become a popular approach. For our book publishing platform, utilizing a monorepo can streamline development, improve code sharing, and simplify dependency management across different packages.

A monorepo is a single repository that contains multiple packages or projects, often related and interdependent. Instead of maintaining separate repositories for each package, all code resides in one repository, facilitating easier collaboration and consistency. In our platform, we might have separate packages for the frontend application, backend API, shared utilities, and various services like authentication and payment processing.

Benefits of Monorepos

- Shared code can be easily accessed and updated across packages without the need for publishing and versioning.
- Dependencies between packages are managed within the repository, reducing conflicts and duplication.
- Developers follow the same processes and tooling across all packages.
- Changes affecting multiple packages can be committed together, ensuring compatibility.

Setting up Monorepo with Yarn Workspaces

To manage multiple packages effectively, we can use tools like Yarn Workspaces or npm Workspaces. Yarn Workspaces allow us to work with multiple packages and handle their dependencies efficiently.

Initialize the Root Repository

Start by creating a new directory for the monorepo and initializing it.

```
mkdir book-publishing-platform
cd book-publishing-platform
yarn init -y
```

This creates a **package.json** file at the root of the repository.

Configure Yarn Workspaces

In the root **package.json**, add the **workspaces** field to specify where the packages are located.

```
{
  "private": true,
  "name": "book-publishing-platform",
  "version": "1.0.0",
  "workspaces": ["packages/*"]
}
```

Here, setting **"private": true** prevents accidental publishing of the root package.

Create Package Directories

Create a **packages** directory to hold all individual packages.

```
mkdir packages
Within packages, create subdirectories for each package.
cd packages
mkdir frontend backend utils
```

Initialize Individual Packages

For each package, initialize it with its own **package.json**.

```
cd frontend
yarn init -y
cd ../backend
yarn init -y
cd ../utils
yarn init -y
```

Define Package Dependencies

Suppose the **backend** package depends on the **utils** package. In the **backend/package.json**, declare this dependency.

```
{
  "name": "backend",
  "version": "1.0.0",
  "dependencies": {
    "utils": "1.0.0"
  }
}
```

Yarn Workspaces will link the **utils** package locally, allowing the **backend** package to use it without publishing to NPM.

Install Dependencies

From the root directory, run:

```
yarn install
```

Yarn will install all dependencies for each workspace and create symlinks between them. Shared dependencies are hoisted to the root **node_modules** to avoid duplication.

Implementing Code Sharing Between Packages

With the workspace set up, we can now share code between packages.

Creating the Utils Package

In **packages/utils**, add functionality that other packages can use.

```
// file: packages/utils/index.js
function formatTitle(title) {
  return title.trim().replace(/\s+/g, ' ').toUpperCase();
}
module.exports = {
  formatTitle,
};
```

Using Utils in Backend Package

In **packages/backend**, require the **utils** package.

```
// file: packages/backend/app.js
const { formatTitle } = require('utils');
const title = formatTitle('  The Great Gatsby  ');
console.log(`Formatted Title: ${title}`);
```

Running the Backend Application

From the **packages/backend** directory, execute:

```
node app.js
```

It should output:

```
Formatted Title: THE GREAT GATSBY
```

Managing External Dependencies

If multiple packages depend on the same external module, Yarn Workspaces hoist the dependency to the root, saving space and ensuring consistent versions.

For example, if both **frontend** and **backend** use **lodash**, declare it in each package:

```
# In packages/frontend
yarn add lodash
# In packages/backend
yarn add lodash
```

After running **yarn install** at the root, **lodash** will be installed once in the root **node_modules**. Then, define scripts in the root **package.json** to streamline development.

```
{
  // Previous fields
  "scripts": {
    "start:backend": "yarn workspace backend start",
    "start:frontend": "yarn workspace frontend start",
    "build": "yarn workspaces run build"
  }
}
```

In each package's **package.json**, define their own scripts.

- Backend Package:

```
{
  // Previous fields
  "scripts": {
    "start": "node app.js",
    "build": "echo Building backend..."
  }
```

```
}
```

- Frontend Package:

```
{
  // Previous fields
  "scripts": {
    "start": "react-scripts start",
    "build": "react-scripts build"
  }
}
```

Now, running **yarn start:backend** from the root will start the backend application.

Handling Versioning within Monorepo

Since all packages are within the same repository, versioning can be managed collectively or individually.

- Collective Versioning: All packages share the same version number.
- Individual Versioning: Each package maintains its own version.

There are varopis tools like Lerna that can assist in managing versioning and publishing within monorepos. Lerna is a tool that optimizes workflow around managing multi-package repositories.

Install Lerna

From the root directory:

```
yarn add lerna -D
npx lerna init
```

Lerna will create a **lerna.json** file.

Configure Lerna

In **lerna.json**, specify the use of Yarn Workspaces.

```
{
  "packages": ["packages/*"],
  "version": "1.0.0",
```

```
  "npmClient": "yarn",
  "useWorkspaces": true
}
```

Lerna can link packages and install dependencies.

```
npx lerna bootstrap
```

Lerna can automate versioning and publishing processes.

```
npx lerna publish
```

Implementing Shared Configurations

First, create a **config** directory at the root for shared configurations.

```
// file: config/.eslintrc.json
{
  "extends": "eslint:recommended",
  "env": {
    "node": true,
    "es6": true
  }
}
```

In each package, reference the shared configuration.

```
// file: packages/backend/package.json
{
  // Previous fields
  "eslintConfig": {
    "extends": "../../config/.eslintrc.json"
  }
}
```

When updating a dependency used by multiple packages, update it at the root.

```
yarn add lodash@latest -W
```

The **-W** or **--ignore-workspace-root-check** flag tells Yarn to add the dependency to the workspace root.

Handling CI/CD Pipelines

It is essential that your Continuous Integration pipelines recognize the monorepo structure.

- Cache the root node_modules directory to accelerate builds.
- Exclude tests for packages that have not changed.

Below is a quick example of GitHub Actions Workflow:

```
# file: .github/workflows/ci.yml
name: CI
on:
  push:
    branches: [main]
jobs:
  build:
    runs-on: ubuntu-latest
    steps:
      - uses: actions/checkout@v2
      - name: Set up Node.js
        uses: actions/setup-node@v2
        with:
          node-version: '14'
      - name: Install dependencies
        run: yarn install --frozen-lockfile
      - name: Run tests
        run: yarn workspaces run test
```

We learned that tools like Yarn Workspaces and Lerna are essential for streamlining development, improving code sharing and simplifying dependency management in our book publishing platform. This approach is the most effective way to ensure better collaboration among team members, maintain consistency across packages and enhance the scalability and maintainability of the application.

Leveraging Native Modules

Understanding Native Modules

Native modules are the solution for extending the capabilities of applications. They allow integration with code written in languages like C or C++. These modules, often called "add-ons," give developers access to more than just JavaScript, offering performance improvements and access to system-level features. Leveraging native modules, we will enhance our book publishing platform with advanced features such as image processing, cryptographic functions, and database operations.

Native modules are dynamic, shared objects that can be loaded into Node.js using the **require()** function. Typically written in C or C++ and compiled to binary format, they are the optimal choice for executing resource-intensive tasks. Node.js offers multiple methods for creating and integrating native modules, including Native Abstractions for Node.js (NAN) and Node-API (N-API), which provide a stable interface for module development.

Popular Native Modules

Some of the widely used native modules in the Node.js ecosystem include:

- **bcrypt**: A module for password hashing, providing secure and efficient encryption.
- **sharp**: An image processing library for resizing, cropping, and converting images.
- **node-sass**: A module that allows the use of Sass stylesheets, compiling them to CSS.
- **better-sqlite3**: A performant SQLite3 wrapper for Node.js applications.
- **grpc**: A high-performance, open-source universal RPC framework.
- **serialport**: A module for accessing serial ports for hardware communication.

Using 'Sharp' Module for Image Processing

To enhance our book publishing platform, we can integrate the **sharp** module for image processing. This allows us to handle tasks like resizing book cover images, generating thumbnails, and converting image formats efficiently.

Installing Sharp Module

First, we need to install the **sharp** module. Since it includes native code, the installation process may involve compiling the module for the target system.

```
npm install sharp
```

The installation script will download pre-compiled binaries for common platforms. If binaries are not available for the system, it will attempt to compile from source, which requires build tools like **node-gyp**, Python, and a C/C++ compiler.

Processing Images with Sharp

Suppose authors upload high-resolution book cover images that need to be resized for optimal display on the website. Using **sharp**, we can automate this process.

```
// file: services/imageService.js
const sharp = require('sharp');
const path = require('path');
function processCoverImage(inputPath, outputPath) {
  return sharp(inputPath)
    .resize(800, 600, {
      fit: sharp.fit.cover,
      position: sharp.strategy.entropy,
    })
    .toFormat('jpeg')
    .jpeg({ quality: 80 })
    .toFile(outputPath)
    .then((info) => {
      console.log('Image processed:', info);
      return info;
    })
    .catch((error) => {
      console.error('Error processing image:', error);
      throw error;
    });
}
module.exports = {
  processCoverImage,
```

```
};
```

Using Image Service in Application

When an author uploads a cover image, we invoke the image processing function.

```
// file: controllers/bookController.js
const { processCoverImage } =
require('../services/imageService');
const path = require('path');
function uploadCoverImage(req, res) {
  const inputPath = req.file.path;
  const outputPath = path.join('uploads', 'covers',
`${req.file.filename}-processed.jpg`);
  processCoverImage(inputPath, outputPath)
    .then(() => {
      res.json({ message: 'Cover image uploaded and processed
successfully' });
    })
    .catch((error) => {
      res.status(500).json({ error: 'Failed to process cover
image' });
    });
}
module.exports = {
  uploadCoverImage,
};
```

Handling Native Module Dependencies

Since native modules may require compilation, it's essential to ensure that the build environment is correctly set up, especially when deploying to different platforms.

Prerequisites for Native Module Compilation

- Ensure that the Node.js version is compatible with the module.
- Node-gyp requires Python 2.7 or Python 3 for building native modules.
- A compatible compiler is needed to compile the native code.

Automating Build Environments

To simplify deployment, let us use Docker to create consistent build environments. Following is the sample Dockerfile for the application:

```
# Use the official Node.js 14 image
FROM node:14
# Install build tools for native modules
RUN apt-get update && apt-get install -y build-essential
python3
# Set the working directory
WORKDIR /app
# Copy package files and install dependencies
COPY package*.json ./
RUN npm install
# Copy the application code
COPY . .
# Expose the application port
EXPOSE 3000
# Start the application
CMD ["npm", "start"]
```

Using Native Modules

For secure password storage, we can use **bcrypt**, which provides a native implementation for efficient hashing.

```
npm install bcrypt
```

Following is a quick implementation of bcrypt for User Authentication:

```
// file: services/authService.js
const bcrypt = require('bcrypt');
```

```
function hashPassword(plainPassword) {
  const saltRounds = 10;
  return bcrypt.hash(plainPassword, saltRounds);
}
function comparePassword(plainPassword, hashedPassword) {
  return bcrypt.compare(plainPassword, hashedPassword);
}
module.exports = {
  hashPassword,
  comparePassword,
};
```

Then we integrating into User Registration:

```
// file: controllers/userController.js
const { hashPassword } = require('../services/authService');
function registerUser(req, res) {
  const { username, password } = req.body;
  hashPassword(password)
    .then((hashedPassword) => {
      // Save user with hashed password
      const user = new User({ username, password:
hashedPassword });
      return user.save();
    })
    .then(() => {
      res.json({ message: 'User registered successfully' });
    })
    .catch((error) => {
      res.status(500).json({ error: 'Registration failed' });
    });
```

```
}
module.exports = {
  registerUser,
};
```

Creating Custom Native Modules Using Node-API (N-API)

For specialized functionality or performance-critical sections, we might consider developing custom native modules. Here, Node-API provides a stable interface for creating native addons.

To begin with,

- Setup the Module Structure

Create a new directory for the module.

```
mkdir native-addon
cd native-addon
npm init -y
```

- Install Development Dependencies

```
npm install --save-dev node-addon-api
```

- Create the C++ Source File

```
// file: addon.cpp
#include <napi.h>
Napi::String Method(const Napi::CallbackInfo& info) {
  Napi::Env env = info.Env();
  return Napi::String::New(env, "Hello from the native
module!");
}
Napi::Object Init(Napi::Env env, Napi::Object exports) {
  exports.Set(Napi::String::New(env, "hello"),
Napi::Function::New(env, Method));
  return exports;
}
```

```
NODE_API_MODULE(addon, Init)
```

- Configure the Build with **binding.gyp**

```
{
  "targets": [
    {
      "target_name": "addon",
      "sources": ["addon.cpp"],
      "cflags!": ["-fno-exceptions"],
      "cflags_cc!": ["-fno-exceptions"],
      "include_dirs": ["<!@(node -p \"require('node-addon-api').include\")"],
      "dependencies": ["<!(node -p \"require('node-addon-api').gyp\")"],
      "defines": ["NAPI_DISABLE_CPP_EXCEPTIONS"]
    }
  ]
}
```

- Build the Addon

Here, use **node-gyp** to build the native module.

```
npm install --global node-gyp
node-gyp configure
node-gyp build
```

The benefits of using native modules are significant. They introduce additional considerations, yes, but their performance and capabilities justify their use. If we understand how to integrate and manage them, we can build more efficient and feature-rich applications.

Dependency Injection and Modular Design Patterns

Understanding Dependency Injection

In building scalable and maintainable applications, implementing dependency injection and modular design patterns is essential. These strategies help in writing code that is loosely coupled, easier to test, and more adaptable to changes. In our book publishing platform, adopting these techniques enhances the overall architecture, making the application robust and maintainable.

Dependency injection (DI) is a design pattern where an object receives other objects it depends on, called dependencies, from an external source rather than creating them internally. This approach decouples the implementation of a class from its dependencies, allowing for greater flexibility and easier testing.

Following are the benefits of Dependency Injection:

- Components are less dependent on concrete implementations.
- Dependencies can be mocked or stubbed during testing.
- Easier to swap out implementations without modifying dependent code.
- Simplifies the codebase by managing dependencies centrally.

Implementing Dependency Injection

While Node.js does not have a built-in DI framework, we can implement dependency injection manually or use libraries like **awilix**, **inversify**, or **typedi**. For our sample program, we'll demonstrate manual dependency injection to understand the core concepts.

Refactoring Code for Dependency Injection

Consider the **userService** that depends on a **userRepository** for data access.

- Without Dependency Injection:

```
// file: services/userService.js
const userRepository =
require('../repositories/userRepository');
function createUser(userData) {
  return userRepository.save(userData);
}
module.exports = {
  createUser,
};
```

In this example, **userService** directly requires **userRepository**, creating a tight coupling. Testing

userService in isolation becomes challenging because it always uses the actual **userRepository**.

- With Dependency Injection:

```
// file: services/userService.js
function createUser(userRepository, userData) {
  return userRepository.save(userData);
}
module.exports = {
  createUser,
};
```

By passing **userRepository** as a parameter, we decouple **userService** from the concrete implementation of **userRepository**.

Injecting Dependencies in the Application

In the application layer, we manage the instantiation and injection of dependencies.

```
// file: app.js
const userRepository =
require('./repositories/userRepository');
const userServiceModule = require('./services/userService');
function main() {
  const userService = {
    createUser: (userData) =>
userServiceModule.createUser(userRepository, userData),
  };
  // Use userService in the application
  userService.createUser({ name: 'Alice', email:
'alice@example.com' })
    .then((user) => {
      console.log('User created:', user);
    })
    .catch((error) => {
```

```
        console.error('Error creating user:', error);
      });
  }
  main();
```

By controlling the creation and injection of dependencies in one place, we enhance flexibility and testability.

Implementing Dependency Injection in Controllers

In Express.js controllers, we can inject services as dependencies.

```
// file: controllers/userController.js
function createUserController(userService) {
  return (req, res) => {
    userService.createUser(req.body)
      .then((user) => res.status(201).json(user))
      .catch((error) => res.status(500).json({ error:
error.message }));
  };
}
module.exports = {
  createUserController,
};
```

Then we are setting up the Controller with Dependencies:

```
// file: routes/userRoutes.js
const express = require('express');
const { createUserController } =
require('../controllers/userController');
const userServiceModule = require('../services/userService');
const userRepository =
require('../repositories/userRepository');
const router = express.Router();
```

```
const userService = {
  createUser: (userData) =>
userServiceModule.createUser(userRepository, userData),
};
router.post('/users', createUserController(userService));
module.exports = router;
```

For testing, we can inject mock repositories to isolate the unit under test.

```
// file: tests/userService.test.js
const { createUser } = require('../services/userService');
test('createUser should save user data', async () => {
  const mockUserRepository = {
    save: jest.fn().mockResolvedValue({ id: 1, name: 'Alice'
}),
  };
  const userData = { name: 'Alice', email: 'alice@example.com'
};
  const result = await createUser(mockUserRepository,
userData);

expect(mockUserRepository.save).toHaveBeenCalledWith(userData)
;
  expect(result).toEqual({ id: 1, name: 'Alice' });
});
```

By injecting a mock **userRepository**, we avoid interacting with the actual database during tests.

Modular Design Patterns

Modular design involves organizing code into separate, interchangeable modules that encapsulate specific functionality. This approach promotes separation of concerns, making the codebase easier to understand and maintain.

Following are the most common modular design patterns:

- Factory Pattern: Creates objects without specifying the exact class of the object to be created.
- Singleton Pattern: Ensures a class has only one instance and provides a global point of access.
- Strategy Pattern: Defines a family of algorithms, encapsulates each one, and makes them interchangeable.
- Observer Pattern: Establishes a subscription mechanism to notify multiple objects about events.

Applying Factory Pattern

In our platform, we might have different database connections based on the environment (development, testing, production). By using the factory pattern, we can create a database connection without exposing the creation logic.

```
// file: factories/dbFactory.js
function createDbConnection(config) {
  if (config.type === 'mysql') {
    // Return MySQL connection
  } else if (config.type === 'postgres') {
    // Return PostgreSQL connection
  } else {
    throw new Error('Unsupported database type');
  }
}
module.exports = {
  createDbConnection,
};
```

Next, using the Factory in the Application:

```
// file: app.js
const { createDbConnection } =
require('./factories/dbFactory');
const config = {
  type: process.env.DB_TYPE || 'mysql',
```

```
  // Other configuration options
};
const dbConnection = createDbConnection(config);
// Inject dbConnection into repositories or services
```

Implementing Singleton Pattern

For resources that should have a single instance throughout the application, like a cache or a configuration manager, we can use the singleton pattern.

```
// file: utils/cache.js
let instance = null;
class Cache {
  constructor() {
    if (!instance) {
      this.store = new Map();
      instance = this;
    }
    return instance;
  }
  set(key, value) {
    this.store.set(key, value);
  }
  get(key) {
    return this.store.get(key);
  }
}
module.exports = Cache;
```

Now, using the Singleton Cache:

```
// file: services/dataService.js
const Cache = require('../utils/cache');
```

```
function fetchData(key) {
  const cache = new Cache();
  let data = cache.get(key);
  if (data) {
    return Promise.resolve(data);
  } else {
    // Fetch data from source
    data = /* ... */;
    cache.set(key, data);
    return Promise.resolve(data);
  }
}
module.exports = {
  fetchData,
};
```

Applying Strategy Pattern

Suppose we have different pricing strategies based on user roles (e.g., regular customer, premium member, wholesale buyer).

Let us first define the Pricing Strategies:

```
// file: strategies/pricingStrategies.js
function regularPricing(price) {
  return price;
}
function premiumPricing(price) {
  return price * 0.9; // 10% discount
}
function wholesalePricing(price) {
  return price * 0.8; // 20% discount
```

```
}
module.exports = {
  regularPricing,
  premiumPricing,
  wholesalePricing,
};
```

Next, implementing the Strategy Selector:

```
// file: services/pricingService.js
const pricingStrategies =
require('../strategies/pricingStrategies');
function getPrice(userRole, basePrice) {
  let strategy;
  switch (userRole) {
    case 'premium':
      strategy = pricingStrategies.premiumPricing;
      break;
    case 'wholesale':
      strategy = pricingStrategies.wholesalePricing;
      break;
    default:
      strategy = pricingStrategies.regularPricing;
  }
  return strategy(basePrice);
}
module.exports = {
  getPrice,
};
```

Now, using the Pricing Service:

```
// file: controllers/orderController.js
const { getPrice } = require('../services/pricingService');
function calculateOrderTotal(req, res) {
  const userRole = req.user.role;
  const basePrice = req.body.basePrice;
  const finalPrice = getPrice(userRole, basePrice);
  res.json({ total: finalPrice });
}
module.exports = {
  calculateOrderTotal,
};
```

Our sample program demonstrates how dependency injection and modular design patterns can be used to create a more testable, maintainable, and adaptable codebase. These strategies promote loose coupling between components, enhance flexibility, and facilitate better testing practices.

Summary

This chapter has provided a comprehensive understanding of Node.js module systems and effective package management. We began our exploration of advanced techniques using Node.js modules, focusing on both CommonJS and ES6 modules. The chapter then moved on to the creation and management of NPM packages. It showed you how to develop custom packages, handle dependencies, and why proper versioning and publishing practices are so important.

Furthermore, the concept of monorepositories and workspace management was introduced. Practical demonstrations showed how to manage multiple packages within a single repository effectively. The advantages of code reusability, simplified dependency management, and streamlined workflows in a monorepo setup are clear when you use tools like Yarn Workspaces and Lerna. The chapter also demonstrated how to leverage native modules to extend the functionality of Node.js applications beyond pure JavaScript. I'll be frank: native modules are the way to handle resource-intensive tasks efficiently.

Finally, we discussed strategies for implementing dependency injection and modular design patterns. These techniques are essential for writing code that is loosely coupled, testable, and maintainable. Practical examples demonstrated how dependency injection and design patterns like Factory, Singleton, and Strategy can improve the architecture of the application, making it more adaptable and easier to manage.

Knowledge Exercise

1. Which of the following statements correctly describes the CommonJS module system in Node.js?

A. It uses **import** and **export** statements and loads modules asynchronously.

B. It uses **require()** and **module.exports** and loads modules synchronously.

C. It is the standardized module system introduced in ECMAScript 2015.

D. It does not support exporting functions or objects from a module.

2. When using ES6 modules in Node.js, how do you enable their usage in your project?

A. By setting **"type": "module"** in **package.json** or using the **.mjs** file extension.

B. By installing a third-party library that adds ES6 module support.

C. By using the **require()** function with ES6 syntax.

D. By transpiling code with Babel before running it in Node.js.

3. What is the primary benefit of organizing code into modules in a Node.js application?

A. It reduces the application's execution time.

B. It allows for code obfuscation to protect intellectual property.

C. It enhances scalability and maintainability by separating concerns.

D. It eliminates the need for external dependencies.

4. Which command initializes a new NPM package and creates a **package.json** file?

A. **npm install**

B. **npm start**

C. **npm init**

D. **npm publish**

5. In the context of NPM packages, what is Semantic Versioning, and how is it formatted?

A. A versioning system using dates in the format **YYYY.MM.DD**.

B. A random numbering system assigned by NPM upon publishing.

C. A versioning scheme formatted as **MAJOR.MINOR.PATCH** indicating compatibility and changes.

D. A system that uses alphabetical letters to denote versions.

6. How can you test an NPM package locally before publishing it to the NPM registry?

A. By using **npm publish --local**.

B. By linking it globally with **npm link** and requiring it in another project.

C. By installing it from GitHub directly.

D. By copying the package files into the **node_modules** directory of another project manually.

7. What is a monorepo in the context of software development?

A. A repository that contains only one package or project.

B. A repository that mirrors another repository.

C. A single repository containing multiple packages or projects, often related and interdependent.

D. A repository that is read-only and cannot be modified.

8. Which tool allows you to manage multiple packages within a monorepo by handling dependencies and linking them locally?

A. NPM Scripts

B. Webpack

C. Yarn Workspaces

D. Git Submodules

9. When integrating a native module like **sharp** into a Node.js application, which of the following is a necessary consideration?

A. Ensuring that the module is written in pure JavaScript.

B. Having a compatible build environment with necessary compilers and tools.

C. Only using the module on Windows operating systems.

D. Modifying the module's source code to match your application's syntax.

10. What is the main advantage of using native modules in a Node.js application?

A. They increase code readability by using C++ syntax.

B. They allow access to system-level features and improve performance for resource-intensive tasks.

C. They make the application platform-independent without additional effort.

D. They automatically update themselves without developer intervention.

11. In dependency injection, what is the primary goal of passing dependencies into modules or classes from an external source?

A. To tightly couple components for faster execution.

B. To reduce the number of files in the codebase.

C. To decouple components, enhancing testability and flexibility.

D. To enforce the use of global variables for shared state.

12. Which of the following is an example of implementing dependency injection in a Node.js module?

A. Requiring all dependencies at the top of the module file.

B. Passing a dependency as a parameter to a function or constructor.

C. Using global variables to access dependencies.

D. Hardcoding dependencies within the functions.

13. What is the Factory Pattern in modular design, and how is it useful?

A. A pattern where objects are created using a new operator directly.

B. A pattern that restricts a class to a single instance.

C. A pattern that provides a way to create objects without specifying the exact class, promoting flexibility.

D. A pattern that allows objects to notify other objects about state changes.

14. In the context of modular design patterns, what is the Singleton Pattern used for?

A. To create multiple instances of a class for scalability.

B. To ensure a class has only one instance and provide a global point of access.

C. To encapsulate a group of individual factories.

D. To define a family of algorithms and make them interchangeable.

15. Why is it advantageous to use dependency injection and modular design patterns together in application development?

A. Because it simplifies the code by combining all components into a single module.

B. Because it eliminates the need for testing individual components.

C. Because it creates a tightly coupled architecture, improving performance.

D. Because it results in a decoupled architecture, enhancing maintainability and testability.

Answers and Explanations

1. B. It uses **require()** and **module.exports** and loads modules synchronously.

CommonJS is the original module system in Node.js, utilizing **require()** to import modules and **module.exports** or **exports** to export them. Modules are loaded synchronously.

2. A. By setting **"type": "module"** in **package.json** or using the **.mjs** file extension.

Enabling ES6 modules in Node.js requires specifying **"type": "module"** in **package.json** or using the **.mjs** file extension to indicate that files should be treated as ES6 modules.

3. C. It enhances scalability and maintainability by separating concerns.

Organizing code into modules allows developers to separate concerns, making the application more scalable and easier to maintain.

4. C. **npm init**

The **npm init** command initializes a new NPM package and creates a **package.json** file with the package's metadata.

5. C. A versioning scheme formatted as **MAJOR.MINOR.PATCH** indicating compatibility and changes.

Semantic Versioning uses the format **MAJOR.MINOR.PATCH**, where each segment signifies the level of changes made, aiding in dependency management and compatibility.

6. B. By linking it globally with **npm link** and requiring it in another project.

Using **npm link** allows you to link your package globally and then use it in another project as if it were installed from NPM, facilitating local testing.

7. C. A single repository containing multiple packages or projects, often related and interdependent.

A monorepo contains multiple packages within one repository, simplifying collaboration and dependency management among related projects.

8. C. Yarn Workspaces

Yarn Workspaces enable the management of multiple packages in a monorepo by handling dependencies and linking packages locally.

9. B. Having a compatible build environment with necessary compilers and tools.

Integrating native modules often requires compiling code, so a compatible build environment with the necessary tools is essential.

10. B. They allow access to system-level features and improve performance for resource-intensive tasks.

Native modules can execute code written in languages like C or C++, providing performance benefits and access to low-level system features.

11. C. To decouple components, enhancing testability and flexibility.

Dependency injection aims to decouple components by injecting dependencies from external sources, making code more testable and flexible.

12. B. Passing a dependency as a parameter to a function or constructor.

By passing dependencies as parameters, modules or classes do not need to know the concrete implementation of their dependencies, facilitating dependency injection.

13. C. A pattern that provides a way to create objects without specifying the exact class, promoting flexibility.

The Factory Pattern abstracts the object creation process, allowing for more flexible and interchangeable object creation.

14. B. To ensure a class has only one instance and provide a global point of access.

The Singleton Pattern restricts a class to a single instance, providing a global access point, which is useful for shared resources like configuration managers.

15. D. Because it results in a decoupled architecture, enhancing maintainability and testability.

Using dependency injection alongside modular design patterns creates a decoupled architecture, making the application easier to maintain and test.

CHAPTER 3: PROCESS MANAGEMENT AND SYSTEM INTERACTION

Overview

In this chapter, we'll take a look at some of the more advanced features of Node.js for managing processes and interacting with the underlying system. We'll start by looking at how to use child processes and clustering to improve application performance and scalability. Once you've got a handle on creating and managing child processes, you can run tasks in parallel, make use of multiple CPU cores, and give your applications a boost.

Next, we'll take a look at how different processes can communicate and share data effectively using inter-process communication methods. This also covers techniques for messaging between processes, which is key for building complex, distributed systems. We'll also show you how to optimize your applications with worker threads. This lets you run CPU-intensive tasks without blocking the main event loop. We'll also talk about environment variables and system resource management. You'll learn how to access and manage environment variables securely, configure your applications for different environments, and interact with system resources.

Finally, we'll look at advanced logging techniques using console and debug modules to monitor application behavior and troubleshoot issues effectively. By implementing robust logging, you can gain insights into your application's performance and quickly identify and resolve problems.

Harnessing Child Processes and Clustering

If you can manage child processes, your application can do more at once. This lets you use multiple CPU cores and make your whole system run faster. By letting child processes do the heavy lifting, we can keep the main process responsive and avoid slowing it down. This is especially helpful in our book publishing platform when we're dealing with tasks like generating PDF previews, processing large data files, or performing complex computations.

Creating and Managing Child Processes

Node.js provides the **child_process** module, which offers methods to spawn child processes. The most commonly used methods are **spawn**, **exec**, and **fork**.

Using 'spawn'

The **spawn** function launches a new process with a given command.

```
const { spawn } = require('child_process');
const ls = spawn('ls', ['-lh', '/usr']);
ls.stdout.on('data', (data) => {
  console.log(`Output: ${data}`);
```

```
});
ls.stderr.on('data', (data) => {
  console.error(`Error: ${data}`);
});
ls.on('close', (code) => {
  console.log(`Child process exited with code ${code}`);
});
```

In this example, it executes the **ls -lh /usr** command. It listens to **stdout**, **stderr**, and the **close** event to handle output and process termination.

Using 'exec'

The **exec** function runs a command in a shell and buffers the output.

```
const { exec } = require('child_process');
exec('cat largefile.txt', (error, stdout, stderr) => {
  if (error) {
    console.error(`Execution error: ${error}`);
    return;
  }
  console.log(`Output: ${stdout}`);
});
```

What we're trying to do here is, that it runs the cat command to read a file. And, it also deals with any errors and sends the output via a callback.

Using 'fork'

The **fork** function is a special case of **spawn** used to create new Node.js processes.

```
const { fork } = require('child_process');
const child = fork('child.js');
child.on('message', (message) => {
  console.log(`Received from child: ${message}`);
});
```

```
child.send({ task: 'start' });
```

In **child.js**:

```
process.on('message', (message) => {
  if (message.task === 'start') {
    // Perform task
    process.send('Task completed');
  }
});
```

This function basically creates a new Node.js process and sets up communication between the parent and child processes. It uses **process.send** and **process.on('message')** to communicate between the processes.

Performing Parallel Tasks with Child Processes

To perform tasks in parallel, we can spawn multiple child processes. In our platform, suppose we need to process multiple book files simultaneously.

- Parent Process

```
const { fork } = require('child_process');
const books = ['book1.pdf', 'book2.pdf', 'book3.pdf'];
books.forEach((book) => {
  const child = fork('processBook.js');
  child.send({ file: book });
  child.on('message', (message) => {
    console.log(`Processing of ${book} completed:
${message.status}`);
  });
  child.on('error', (error) => {
    console.error(`Error processing ${book}: ${error}`);
  });
});
```

- Child Process (**processBook.js**)

```
process.on('message', (message) => {
  const file = message.file;
  // Simulate processing
  console.log(`Processing ${file}`);
  setTimeout(() => {
    // Send completion message
    process.send({ status: 'success' });
    process.exit();
  }, 2000);
});
```

This one processes each book file in a separate process. The parent manages the child processes, handling messages and errors.

Clustering for Improved Scalability

Clustering allows a Node.js application to create multiple worker processes that share the same server port. This enables the application to handle more concurrent connections by distributing requests across multiple processes.

Setting up Clustering

Here, the Node.js provides the **cluster** module to create a cluster of worker processes.

- Master Process

```
const cluster = require('cluster');
const os = require('os');
if (cluster.isMaster) {
  const numCPUs = os.cpus().length;
  console.log(`Master ${process.pid} is running`);
  // Fork workers
  for (let i = 0; i < numCPUs; i++) {
    cluster.fork();
```

```
  }
  cluster.on('exit', (worker, code, signal) => {
    console.log(`Worker ${worker.process.pid} exited`);
    // Optionally, restart the worker
    cluster.fork();
  });
} else {
  // Workers can share any TCP connection
  // In this case, an HTTP server
  const http = require('http');
  http.createServer((req, res) => {
    res.writeHead(200);
    res.end(`Hello from worker ${process.pid}\n`);
  }).listen(8000);
  console.log(`Worker ${process.pid} started`);
}
```

The idea is to have a master process for the forks worker processes, and to have that number be the same as the number of CPU cores. The master listens out for worker exits and can restart them if needed.

Each worker runs the same code as the master, but skips the master-specific code because of the **cluster.isMaster** check. Our workers use the same server port (like, port 8000).

Applying Clustering to Our Platform

In our book publishing platform, we can also use clustering to handle more simultaneous user requests, improving response times and application availability.

Let us consider the example of clustering in an Express.js application:

- Cluster Setup

```
const cluster = require('cluster');
const os = require('os');
const numCPUs = os.cpus().length;
```

```
if (cluster.isMaster) {
  console.log(`Master ${process.pid} is running`);
  for (let i = 0; i < numCPUs; i++) {
    cluster.fork();
  }
  cluster.on('exit', (worker, code, signal) => {
    console.log(`Worker ${worker.process.pid} died`);
    cluster.fork();
  });
} else {
  // Worker processes
  const express = require('express');
  const app = express();
  app.get('/', (req, res) => {
    res.send(`Response from worker ${process.pid}`);
  });
  app.listen(3000, () => {
    console.log(`Worker ${process.pid} started`);
  });
}
```

This one's about setting up an Express.js server with clustering. The master process handles the lifecycles of the workers.

Handling Sticky Sessions

For applications that maintain session state, such as user authentication, it's important to ensure that requests from the same client are handled by the same worker. This is known as sticky sessions.

The solution here is to use a load balancer that supports sticky sessions or to implement shared session storage (like Redis).

Following is an example with shared session storage:

- Install Dependencies

```
npm install express-session connect-redis redis
```

- Configure Shared Sessions

```
const session = require('express-session');
const RedisStore = require('connect-redis')(session);
const redisClient = require('redis').createClient();
app.use(session({
  store: new RedisStore({ client: redisClient }),
  secret: 'your-secret-key',
  resave: false,
  saveUninitialized: false
}));
```

This feature stores session data in Redis, which all worker processes can access. The great thing about this is that users can be served by any worker without losing their session data.

By creating and managing child processes, we can perform parallel tasks without blocking the main event loop. Clustering further enhances scalability by distributing incoming connections across multiple worker processes, fully utilizing the server's resources. In our book publishing platform, these techniques enable us to handle increased user load, process large files, and maintain a responsive user experience.

Inter-Process Communication Methods

In complex applications, enabling efficient communication between processes is crucial for coordinating tasks, sharing data, and ensuring smooth operation. In Node.js, inter-process communication (IPC) allows separate processes to exchange messages and data. Building on the previous topic of harnessing child processes and clustering, we'll explore various methods for enabling communication between processes in our book publishing platform.

Understanding Inter-Process Communication

When using child processes or clusters, processes run independently with their own memory spaces. IPC mechanisms enable these processes to communicate, allowing them to work collaboratively.

Common IPC methods include:

1. Message Passing via **process.send()** and **process.on('message')**
2. Using Built-in IPC Channels in Clusters
3. Leveraging Sockets for Communication
4. Utilizing External Message Brokers (e.g., Redis, RabbitMQ)
5. Shared Memory

Message Passing with process.send() and process.on('message')

When spawning child processes using **fork()**, Node.js sets up a communication channel between the parent and child processes. This channel allows for bidirectional message passing.

Consider the followig an example of Parent and Child Communication:

- Parent Process:

```
// file: parent.js
const { fork } = require('child_process');
const child = fork('child.js');
child.on('message', (message) => {
  console.log(`Parent received: ${message}`);
});
child.send('Hello from parent');
child.on('exit', (code) => {
  console.log(`Child exited with code ${code}`);
});
```

- Child Process:

```
// file: child.js
process.on('message', (message) => {
  console.log(`Child received: ${message}`);
  process.send('Hello from child');
  process.exit();
});
```

When you use **fork()**, a communication channel is automatically set up. To send messages to the other process, use **process.send(message)**, and you can listen for message events with **process.on('message', callback)**.

Suppose we have a child process handling PDF generation for book previews. We can send the book data to the child process and receive status updates as shown below:

- Parent Process (Server):

```
const { fork } = require('child_process');
function generateBookPreview(bookId) {
  const child = fork('pdfGenerator.js');
  child.send({ bookId });
  child.on('message', (message) => {
    if (message.status === 'completed') {
      console.log(`Preview generated for book ${bookId}`);
    } else if (message.status === 'error') {
      console.error(`Error generating preview for book
${bookId}: ${message.error}`);
    }
  });
}
```

- Child Process (pdfGenerator.js):

```
process.on('message', async (message) => {
  const { bookId } = message;
  try {
    // Simulate PDF generation
    await generatePDF(bookId);
    process.send({ status: 'completed' });
  } catch (error) {
    process.send({ status: 'error', error: error.message });
  } finally {
    process.exit();
```

```
  }
});
async function generatePDF(bookId) {
  // Placeholder for actual PDF generation logic
  console.log(`Generating PDF for book ${bookId}`);
  return new Promise((resolve) => setTimeout(resolve, 3000));
}
```

Using Built-in IPC Channels

When using the **cluster** module, worker processes can communicate with the master process via IPC channels.

Following is a quick example on worker reporting metrics to master:

- Master Process:

```
const cluster = require('cluster');
const os = require('os');
if (cluster.isMaster) {
  const numCPUs = os.cpus().length;
  console.log(`Master ${process.pid} is running`);
  const workers = [];
  for (let i = 0; i < numCPUs; i++) {
    const worker = cluster.fork();
    workers.push(worker);
    worker.on('message', (message) => {
      if (message.type === 'request_count') {
        console.log(`Worker ${worker.process.pid} has handled
${message.count} requests`);
      }
    });
  }
```

```
  // Optionally, broadcast messages to workers
  setInterval(() => {
    workers.forEach((worker) => {
      worker.send({ type: 'broadcast', message: 'Keep up the
good work!' });
    });
  }, 5000);
} else {
  const http = require('http');
  let requestCount = 0;
  http.createServer((req, res) => {
    requestCount++;
    res.writeHead(200);
    res.end(`Response from worker ${process.pid}\n`);
    // Report to master
    process.send({ type: 'request_count', count: requestCount
});
  }).listen(8000);
  process.on('message', (message) => {
    if (message.type === 'broadcast') {
      console.log(`Worker ${process.pid} received message:
${message.message}`);
    }
  });
  console.log(`Worker ${process.pid} started`);
}
```

Let's look at how we can improve communication between the master and the workers. Workers can send messages to the master using the **process.send()** function. You can also send messages to everyone in the group by using the **process.send()** function. The master can send messages to a specific worker or to everyone.

Leveraging Sockets for Communication

For more complex communication requirements, processes can communicate via sockets using protocols like TCP or UNIX domain sockets.

Below is an example on using UNIX Domain Sockets:

- Parent Process:

```
const net = require('net');
const { fork } = require('child_process');
const socketPath = '/tmp/app.sock';
// Remove existing socket file
const fs = require('fs');
if (fs.existsSync(socketPath)) {
  fs.unlinkSync(socketPath);
}
const server = net.createServer((connection) => {
  console.log('Client connected');
  connection.on('data', (data) => {
    console.log(`Received: ${data}`);
  });
  connection.write('Hello from parent\n');
});
server.listen(socketPath, () => {
  console.log('Server listening on socket');
  // Fork child process
  const child = fork('socketChild.js');
  child.send({ socketPath });
});
```

- Child Process (socketChild.js):

```
process.on('message', (message) => {
```

```
  const net = require('net');
  const client = net.createConnection({ path:
message.socketPath });
  client.on('connect', () => {
    console.log('Child connected to server');
    client.write('Hello from child\n');
  });
  client.on('data', (data) => {
    console.log(`Child received: ${data}`);
  });
});
```

This establishes a socket connection between processes. You can use it between unrelated processes.

Utilizing External Message Brokers

For distributed systems or when processes are on different machines, using external message brokers like Redis Pub/Sub, RabbitMQ, or ZeroMQ is effective.

Let us take an example using Redis Pub/Sub:

We first install Redis and the redis npm package.

```
npm install redis
```

- Publisher Process:

```
const redis = require('redis');
const publisher = redis.createClient();
setInterval(() => {
  const message = `Update at ${new Date()}`;
  publisher.publish('updates', message);
  console.log(`Published: ${message}`);
}, 2000);
```

- Subscriber Process:

```
const redis = require('redis');
const subscriber = redis.createClient();
subscriber.subscribe('updates');
subscriber.on('message', (channel, message) => {
  console.log(`Received message from ${channel}: ${message}`);
});
```

The idea is to decouple things so that processes can scale independently. The processes are decoupled, so they can scale independently.

By exploring methods like message passing, using IPC channels in clusters, leveraging sockets, and utilizing external message brokers, we can enable processes to work together seamlessly. In our book publishing platform, implementing these IPC methods allows us to coordinate tasks like file processing, notifications, and workload distribution effectively.

Optimizing with Worker Threads

I've found that Node.js is great for I/O-bound operations because of its event loop and single-threaded nature. However, it can be a bit tricky when it comes to CPU-intensive tasks. If you're running heavy computations on the main thread, it can block the event loop, which can lead to decreased performance and unresponsive apps. Node.js version 10.5.0 introduced Worker Threads, which were then stabilized in version 12. These threads let you run CPU-intensive tasks without blocking the main thread.

What Are Worker Threads?

Worker Threads allow you to run JavaScript code in parallel threads, sharing memory efficiently. Unlike child processes, which have separate memory spaces, worker threads share the same memory, enabling faster communication and reduced overhead. They are ideal for offloading heavy computations while keeping the main thread responsive.

Key Features of Worker Threads:

- Run multiple threads concurrently.
- Use **SharedArrayBuffer** to share memory between threads.
- Communicate via messaging or shared memory without significant overhead.
- Workers run within the same process, making resource management simpler.

Worker Threads for CPU-Intensive Tasks

To utilize worker threads, you need to import the **worker_threads** module. Here's how you can implement them in your application.

Setting up a Worker Thread

- Main Thread (Parent):

```
// file: main.js
const { Worker } = require('worker_threads');
function runService(workerData) {
  return new Promise((resolve, reject) => {
    const worker = new Worker('./worker.js', { workerData });
    worker.on('message', resolve);
    worker.on('error', reject);
    worker.on('exit', (code) => {
      if (code !== 0)
        reject(new Error(`Worker stopped with exit code
${code}`));
    });
  });
}
async function run() {
  try {
    const result = await runService(42);
    console.log(`Result: ${result}`);
  } catch (err) {
    console.error(err);
  }
}
run();
```

The main thread (main.js) does three main things:

- It creates a new worker instance, linking it to the worker script.

- It passes data (workerData) to the worker.
- It listens for messages, errors, and exit events from the worker.

- Worker Thread:

```
// file: worker.js
const { parentPort, workerData } = require('worker_threads');
function fibonacci(n) {
  if (n <= 1) return n;
  return fibonacci(n - 1) + fibonacci(n - 2);
}
const result = fibonacci(workerData);
parentPort.postMessage(result);
```

In the Worker Thread (worker.js), the data is accessed using workerData. Then, a CPU-intensive task (calculating Fibonacci numbers) is performed. Finally, the result is sent back to the main thread using parentPort.postMessage().

Performing CPU-Intensive Tasks Without Blocking

By offloading the computation to a worker thread, the main thread remains free to handle other tasks. In the example above, calculating the Fibonacci sequence for large numbers is CPU-intensive. Running this on the main thread would block the event loop.

Suppose our book publishing platform needs to perform text analysis on manuscripts, such as counting word frequency or detecting plagiarism, which are CPU-intensive operations.

- Main Application (**`app.js`**):

```
const express = require('express');
const { Worker } = require('worker_threads');
const app = express();
app.use(express.json());
app.post('/analyze', (req, res) => {
  const manuscript = req.body.text;
  const worker = new Worker('./analyzerWorker.js', {
    workerData: { text: manuscript },
```

```
  });
  worker.on('message', (result) => {
    res.json({ analysis: result });
  });
  worker.on('error', (err) => {
    console.error('Worker error:', err);
    res.status(500).json({ error: 'Analysis failed' });
  });
  worker.on('exit', (code) => {
    if (code !== 0)
      console.error(`Worker stopped with exit code ${code}`);
  });
});
app.listen(3000, () => {
  console.log('Server is running on port 3000');
});
```

- Worker Script (**analyzerWorker.js**):

```
const { parentPort, workerData } = require('worker_threads');
function analyzeText(text) {
  // Simulate heavy computation
  const wordCounts = {};
  const words = text.split(/\s+/);
  for (const word of words) {
    wordCounts[word] = (wordCounts[word] || 0) + 1;
  }
  return wordCounts;
}
const result = analyzeText(workerData.text);
```

```
parentPort.postMessage(result);
```

The client sends us the manuscript text. This creates a worker thread to do the text analysis. The main thread is still ready to handle other requests. Once it's done the analysis, it sends the results back to the client.

Managing Multiple Worker Threads

For handling multiple tasks concurrently, you can create a pool of worker threads or spawn new ones as required.

Let us consider an example of Worker Pool implementation. Now here, to avoid creating too many threads, which can exhaust system resources, implement a worker pool.

```
// file: workerPool.js
const { Worker } = require('worker_threads');
class WorkerPool {
  constructor(numThreads, workerScript) {
    this.numThreads = numThreads;
    this.workerScript = workerScript;
    this.workers = [];
    this.queue = [];
    this.activeWorkers = 0;
    for (let i = 0; i < numThreads; i++) {
      this.workers.push(new Worker(workerScript));
    }
  }
  runTask(task) {
    return new Promise((resolve, reject) => {
      const worker = this.workers.pop();
      if (worker) {
        this.activeWorkers++;
        worker.once('message', (result) => {
          this.activeWorkers--;
```

```
          this.workers.push(worker);
          resolve(result);
          this.next();
        });
        worker.once('error', reject);
        worker.postMessage(task);
      } else {
        this.queue.push({ task, resolve, reject });
      }
    });
  }
  next() {
    if (this.queue.length > 0 && this.workers.length > 0) {
      const { task, resolve, reject } = this.queue.shift();
      this.runTask(task).then(resolve).catch(reject);
    }
  }
}
module.exports = WorkerPool;
```

Here, it manages a set number of worker threads. If all the workers are already busy, the tasks are put on hold until they can be completed. It also sets a limit on the number of threads that can run at once.

Sharing Memory Between Threads

Worker threads can share memory using **SharedArrayBuffer** and **Atomics** for synchronization. Consider the following example of shared memory:

- Main Thread:

```
const { Worker, isMainThread, workerData } =
require('worker_threads');
if (isMainThread) {
```

```
  const sharedBuffer = new SharedArrayBuffer(4);
  const sharedArray = new Int32Array(sharedBuffer);
  const worker = new Worker(__filename, { workerData:
sharedBuffer });
  worker.on('exit', () => {
    console.log(`Final counter value:
${Atomics.load(sharedArray, 0)}`);
  });
} else {
  const sharedArray = new Int32Array(workerData);
  for (let i = 0; i < 1000000; i++) {
    Atomics.add(sharedArray, 0, 1);
  }
}
```

In the above, it creates a shared memory space, and it provides atomic operations to prevent race conditions. It's great for high-performance scenarios that require shared state.

The great thing about our platform is that it lets you integrate worker threads for tasks like text analysis, image processing, or complex computations. This makes the application more efficient and scalable. If you know how to implement and manage worker threads, you can handle demanding workloads without compromising on performance.

Environment Variables and System Resource Management

Understanding Environment Variables

It's really important to manage environment variables and system resources when you're setting up Node.js applications in different environments, like development, testing and production. If you handle things right, you can be sure that sensitive information is safe and that the application works the way it should, even when conditions change.

Environment variables are basically key-value pairs that let you configure apps without hardcoding values into the code. They're often used to store sensitive info like database credentials, API keys, and configuration settings that differ between environments.

Following are the benefits of Environment Variables:

- Keeps sensitive data out of the codebase and version control systems.
- Allows different configurations for development, testing, and production.
- Simplifies updates to configuration without code changes.

Managing Environment Variables in Node.js

Node.js lets you access environment variables through the **process.env** object. Here's how you can use them:

Setting Environment Variables

- Directly in the Shell:

```
export PORT=3000
node app.js
```

- Using a **.env** file:

Create a **.env** file in the root of your project:

```
PORT=3000
DB_HOST=localhost
DB_USER=myuser
DB_PASS=mypassword
```

Install the **dotenv** package to load variables from the **.env** file:

```
npm install dotenv
```

In your application entry point **(app.js)**, load the environment variables:

```
require('dotenv').config();
```

Using Environment Variables

```
// file: app.js
require('dotenv').config();
const express = require('express');
const app = express();
```

```
const PORT = process.env.PORT || 8000;
app.listen(PORT, () => {
  console.log(`Server is running on port ${PORT}`);
});
```

Securely Managing .env file

- Add .env to .gitignore

Ensure the .env file is not committed to version control.

```
# file: .gitignore
node_modules/
.env
```

- Use Environment-Specific **.env** files

Create files like **.env.development**, **.env.production**, and load them based on the environment.

```
// file: app.js
const dotenv = require('dotenv');
const env = process.env.NODE_ENV || 'development';
dotenv.config({ path: `.env.${env}` });
```

Setting 'NODE_ENV'

- In Development

```
export NODE_ENV=development
node app.js
```

- In Production

```
export NODE_ENV=production
node app.js
```

System Resource Management

Managing system resources involves configuring how the application uses memory, CPU, and other system resources. Proper management ensures optimal performance and prevents resource exhaustion.

Controlling Resource Usage

- Limiting Memory Usage:

Use the **--max-old-space-size** flag to limit the V8 heap size (in megabytes):

```
node --max-old-space-size=1024 app.js
```

It prevents the application from using more than the specified memory, which can help identify memory leaks.

Monitoring Resource Usage

Utilize modules like **pidusage** to monitor CPU and memory usage:

```
npm install pidusage
```

Below is an example:

```
const pidusage = require('pidusage');
setInterval(() => {
  pidusage(process.pid, (err, stats) => {
    console.log(`CPU Usage: ${stats.cpu}%`);
    console.log(`Memory Usage: ${stats.memory / 1024 / 1024}
MB`);
  });
}, 5000);
```

Handling Uncaught Exceptions and Rejections

Implement handlers to catch unexpected errors and prevent crashes:

```
process.on('uncaughtException', (error) => {
  console.error('Uncaught Exception:', error);
  // Optionally restart the application or perform cleanup
});
process.on('unhandledRejection', (reason, promise) => {
```

```
  console.error('Unhandled Rejection at:', promise, 'reason:',
reason);
  // Handle the rejection
});
```

Graceful Shutdown

Handle termination signals to perform cleanup before exiting:

```
process.on('SIGTERM', () => {
  console.log('Received SIGTERM, shutting down gracefully');
  server.close(() => {
    console.log('Closed out remaining connections');
    process.exit(0);
  });
});
```

This ensures that ongoing requests are completed and resources are released properly.

Configuring Application Behavior

Let us consider the following example on Logging Levels wherein we adjust the logging verbosity based on the environment:

```
const winston = require('winston');
const logger = winston.createLogger({
  level: process.env.NODE_ENV === 'production' ? 'warn' :
'debug',
  transports: [
    new winston.transports.Console(),
  ],
});
module.exports = logger;


const logger = require('./logger');
```

```
logger.debug('This is a debug message');
logger.warn('This is a warning message');
```

In development, we're showing all logs, including debug messages. And in production, we're only logging warnings and errors.

Application Configuration Management

It's a good idea to use a central configuration module to manage environment variables and default values.

- Configuration Module (**config.js**):

```
// file: config.js
require('dotenv').config();
module.exports = {
  port: process.env.PORT || 3000,
  db: {
    host: process.env.DB_HOST || 'localhost',
    user: process.env.DB_USER || 'defaultuser',
    pass: process.env.DB_PASS || 'defaultpass',
  },
  apiKeys: {
    paymentGateway: process.env.PAYMENT_GATEWAY_API_KEY,
  },
  environment: process.env.NODE_ENV || 'development',
};
```

Now let us use the Configuration Module in below:

```
const config = require('./config');
app.listen(config.port, () => {
  console.log(`Server is running in ${config.environment} mode
on port ${config.port}`);
});
```

If we manage our environment variables and system resources effectively, we can set up our Node.js application securely for different environments. Using these practices in our book publishing platform makes it more secure, easier to maintain, and scalable, which gives us a solid foundation for ongoing development and deployment.

Advanced Logging with Console and Debug Modules

Importance of Logging

It's important to have good logging in place so you can keep an eye on how an application is working, spot any problems and make sure the system is running smoothly. There are some great tools for logging in Node.js, including the built-in **console** module and the third-party **debug** module. These can be used to create flexible and informative logging strategies for our book publishing platform.

Logging has a lot of different uses. For example, it helps us find and fix problems when we're developing new things. It also gives us insights into how things work in production. Plus, it records important events, which is useful for compliance and analysis. And it captures errors and exceptions, so we can fix them quickly. When we use more advanced logging, we can control how detailed the logs are, format them for readability, and send them to the right places based on the environment.

Utilizing 'Console' Module

The **console** module is a global object in Node.js that provides simple logging methods:

- **`console.log()`**: Standard output.
- **`console.error()`**: Standard error output.
- **`console.warn()`**: Warning messages.
- **`console.info()`**: Informational messages.
- **`console.debug()`**: Debugging messages (alias for **`console.log()`**).

Following is a simple example on using the **console** modules:

```
console.log('Server started on port 3000');
console.warn('Disk space is running low');
console.error('Failed to connect to the database');
```

While the **console** module is straightforward, it lacks advanced features like log levels, timestamps, and formatting. To enhance its capabilities, we can create a custom logger or use third-party libraries.

Creating a Custom Logger with Console

We can extend the **console** module to include log levels and formatting. Following is one of the custom logger Implementation:

```
// file: logger.js
const util = require('util');
const levels = {
  error: 0,
  warn: 1,
  info: 2,
  debug: 3,
};
let currentLevel = levels.info;
function setLevel(level) {
  if (levels[level] !== undefined) {
    currentLevel = levels[level];
  } else {
    throw new Error(`Invalid log level: ${level}`);
  }
}
function log(level, message, ...args) {
  if (levels[level] <= currentLevel) {
    const timestamp = new Date().toISOString();
    const formattedMessage = util.format(message, ...args);
    console.log(`[${timestamp}] [${level.toUpperCase()}]
${formattedMessage}`);
  }
}
```

```
module.exports = {
  setLevel,
  error: (msg, ...args) => log('error', msg, ...args),
  warn: (msg, ...args) => log('warn', msg, ...args),
  info: (msg, ...args) => log('info', msg, ...args),
  debug: (msg, ...args) => log('debug', msg, ...args),
};
```

Now, let us use the custom logger:

```
// file: app.js
const logger = require('./logger');
// Set log level based on environment
const env = process.env.NODE_ENV || 'development';
if (env === 'development') {
  logger.setLevel('debug');
} else {
  logger.setLevel('info');
}
logger.info('Application started');
logger.debug('Debugging information: %o', { env });
logger.error('An error occurred: %s', 'Database connection
failed');
```

You can adjust how detailed the logs are. You can also set timestamps for each log entry. And while it does, it still uses **util.format()** for string interpolation.

Redirecting Logs to Files

In production, it's often necessary to save logs to files for later analysis as shown below:

```
// file: logger.js
const fs = require('fs');
const util = require('util');
```

```
const logFile = fs.createWriteStream('app.log', { flags: 'a'
});
// Modify the log function
function log(level, message, ...args) {
  if (levels[level] <= currentLevel) {
    const timestamp = new Date().toISOString();
    const formattedMessage = util.format(message, ...args);
    const output = `[${timestamp}] [${level.toUpperCase()}]
${formattedMessage}\n`;
    logFile.write(output);
  }
}
```

Just a couple things to think about:

- One is that it would be good to implement log rotation to keep files from getting out of control.
- And secondly, we need to make sure that logging doesn't get in the way of what the main thread is doing.

Using 'Debug' Module

The **debug** module is a popular library that provides a simple mechanism for conditional logging. See the following example to understand how the **debug** module is put into use:

```
npm install debug
// file: services/userService.js
const debug = require('debug')('app:userService');
function createUser(userData) {
  debug('Creating user with data: %O', userData);
  // User creation logic
}
module.exports = {
  createUser,
```

```
};
```

Set the **DEBUG** environment variable:

```
DEBUG=app:userService node app.js
```

Here are a few wildcard options to help you out:

- DEBUG=app: this one enables all debug logs that start with "app:".
- DEBUG=: This one enables all debug logs.

Integrating Debug into App

For instance, if you wanted to add the "Debug" option to your "Controllers" and "Services" sections, you'd just do that!

- User Controller (controllers/userController.js):

```
const debug = require('debug')('app:userController');
const userService = require('../services/userService');
function registerUser(req, res) {
  const userData = req.body;
  debug('Received registration data: %O', userData);
  userService.createUser(userData)
    .then((user) => {
      debug('User created: %O', user);
      res.status(201).json(user);
    })
    .catch((error) => {
      debug('Error creating user: %O', error);
      res.status(500).json({ error: error.message });
    });
}
module.exports = {
  registerUser,
};
```

- Book Service (services/bookService.js):

```
const debug = require('debug')('app:bookService');
function addNewBook(bookData) {
  debug('Adding new book: %O', bookData);
  // Book creation logic
}
module.exports = {
  addNewBook,
};
DEBUG=app:userController,app:bookService node app.js
DEBUG=app:* node app.js
```

Combining Console and Debug Modules

While **console** provides general logging capabilities, **debug** offers conditional logging with minimal performance impact. Combining both allows for comprehensive logging strategies. For instance, we use the Console for important logs and the Debug mode for the more verbose logs.

- Error Handling Middleware (middleware):

```
const logger = require('../logger');
function errorHandler(err, req, res, next) {
  logger.error('Unhandled error: %s', err.message);
  res.status(500).json({ error: 'Internal Server Error' });
}
module.exports = errorHandler;
```

- Application Entry Point (app.js):

```
const express = require('express');
const errorHandler = require('./middleware/errorHandler');
const userRoutes = require('./routes/userRoutes');
const app = express();
app.use(express.json());
```

```
app.use('/users', userRoutes);
// Other routes and middleware
app.use(errorHandler);
app.listen(3000, () => {
  console.log('Server is running on port 3000');
});
```

Using the console and debug modules to set up some advanced logging lets us keep an eye on and maintain the Node.js application more easily. By tailoring the logging approach to suit different environments and requirements, we can gain useful insights into how the application behaves. This helps us identify and resolve issues quickly and make sure that our book publishing platform runs smoothly for users.

Summary

To sum up this chapter, we delved into advanced Node.js concepts focusing on process management and system interaction. We began by exploring how to harness child processes and implement clustering to enhance application performance. By creating and managing child processes, we were able to execute tasks in parallel, utilizing multiple CPU cores and improving efficiency.

Next, we examined inter-process communication methods to enable effective data sharing between processes. We learned about various techniques such as message passing using **process.send()** and **process.on('message')**, leveraging built-in IPC channels in clusters, and utilizing sockets and external message brokers like Redis. We then focused on optimizing applications using worker threads. We practiced implementing worker threads to handle heavy computations, which enhanced performance without compromising the non-blocking nature of Node.js.

Managing environment variables and system resources was another critical aspect we covered. We learned how to securely configure applications for different environments by using environment variables and the **dotenv** module. This included handling sensitive information like API keys and database credentials without exposing them in the codebase. Additionally, we explored system resource management techniques such as monitoring CPU and memory usage, handling uncaught exceptions, and implementing graceful shutdown procedures to ensure application stability.

And then finally, we delved into advanced logging mechanisms using the console and debug modules. By implementing custom loggers and utilizing third-party libraries like **debug** and **winston**, we enhanced our ability to monitor application behavior and troubleshoot issues effectively. We practiced setting up different logging levels, formatting log messages, redirecting logs to files, and integrating with monitoring tools. This comprehensive logging strategy enabled us to gain valuable insights into our applications, facilitating proactive maintenance and timely error resolution.

Knowledge Exercise

1. Which Node.js module is used to create child processes that can execute commands or scripts in parallel?

A. **cluster**

B. **child_process**

C. **worker_threads**

D. **process**

2. What is the primary purpose of using the **fork()** method from the **child_process** module?

A. To execute shell commands asynchronously

B. To spawn a new Node.js process and set up communication with it

C. To create a new thread within the same process

D. To clone the current process memory

3. In the context of Node.js clustering, what is the role of the master process?

A. To handle all incoming HTTP requests directly

B. To distribute incoming connections to worker processes

C. To perform CPU-intensive tasks

D. To manage environment variables

4. How do worker processes communicate with the master process when using the **cluster** module?

A. Through shared memory

B. By sending signals like **SIGINT**

C. Via built-in inter-process communication (IPC) channels using **process.send()** and **process.on('message')**

D. They cannot communicate; workers are isolated

5. Which method allows Node.js processes to communicate over sockets, enabling communication between unrelated processes?

A. Using **process.send()** and **process.on('message')**

B. Utilizing UNIX domain sockets with the **net** module

C. Employing the **cluster** module's IPC

D. Accessing shared variables between processes

6. What is the main advantage of using worker threads in Node.js?

A. They allow for non-blocking I/O operations

B. They enable execution of CPU-intensive tasks without blocking the event loop

C. They provide a way to create new processes with separate memory spaces

D. They replace the need for asynchronous programming

7. Which module in Node.js provides the functionality to create worker threads?

A. **cluster**

B. **child_process**

C. **worker_threads**

D. **os**

8. When managing environment variables in a Node.js application, which package is commonly used to load variables from a **.env** file?

A. **dotenv**

B. **env-loader**

C. **config**

D. **environment**

9. How can you prevent sensitive information in a **.env** file from being committed to a Git repository?

A. By encrypting the **.env** file

B. By adding **.env** to the **.gitignore** file

C. By storing the **.env** file in a separate folder

D. By renaming the **.env** file to **config.js**

10. What is the purpose of setting the **NODE_ENV** environment variable in a Node.js application?

A. To specify the port number the application should run on

B. To determine the type of database to connect to

C. To define the environment (development, production, etc.) and enable environment-specific configurations

D. To set the maximum memory usage of the application

11. Which of the following is NOT a recommended practice for managing environment variables and system resources securely?

A. Hardcoding sensitive information directly into the code

B. Using environment variables to store configuration data

C. Loading different **.env** files based on the environment

D. Adding the **.env** file to **.gitignore**

12. In Node.js, what is the main benefit of using the **debug** module over the built-in **console.log** for logging?

A. It automatically writes logs to files

B. It allows for conditional logging based on namespaces, reducing performance overhead when logs are disabled

C. It formats logs in JSON for easy parsing

D. It provides built-in log rotation

13. How do you enable debug messages from the **debug** module for a specific namespace when running your Node.js application?

A. By setting the **DEBUG** environment variable to the desired namespace

B. By calling **debug.enable('namespace')** in your code

C. By passing a command-line argument **--debug=namespace**

D. By setting **process.env.NODE_DEBUG** to **true**

14. What is the primary use of the **process.on('uncaughtException', callback)** event handler in a Node.js application?

A. To handle all promise rejections

B. To catch exceptions in asynchronous code

C. To handle exceptions that are not caught elsewhere and prevent the application from crashing abruptly

D. To manage system signals like **SIGINT**

15. When using the **worker_threads** module, which object is used within the worker thread to communicate back to the parent thread?

A. **process**

B. **parentPort**

C. **workerData**

D. **childProcess**

Answers and Explanations

1. B. **child_process**

The **child_process** module provides methods to create child processes (**spawn**, **exec**, **fork**, etc.) that can execute commands or scripts in parallel.

2. B. To spawn a new Node.js process and set up communication with it

The **fork()** method is used to create a new Node.js child process and establishes an IPC channel for communication between the parent and child processes.

3. B. To distribute incoming connections to worker processes

In clustering, the master process listens for incoming connections and distributes them to the worker processes for handling.

4. C. Via built-in inter-process communication (IPC) channels using **process.send()** and **process.on('message')**

Workers and the master process communicate using IPC channels provided by Node.js, typically using **process.send()** to send messages and **process.on('message')** to receive them.

5. B. Utilizing UNIX domain sockets with the **net** module

Sockets created using the **net** module (e.g., UNIX domain sockets) allow processes, including unrelated ones, to communicate over network interfaces or local sockets.

6. B. They enable execution of CPU-intensive tasks without blocking the event loop

Worker threads allow CPU-bound tasks to run in parallel threads, preventing them from blocking the main event loop and keeping the application responsive.

7. C. **worker_threads**

The **worker_threads** module provides the functionality to create and manage worker threads in Node.js.

8. A. **dotenv**

The **dotenv** package loads environment variables from a **.env** file into **process.env**, making it easy to manage configuration settings.

9. B. By adding **.env** to the **.gitignore** file

Adding **.env** to **.gitignore** ensures that the file is not tracked by Git and prevents sensitive information from being committed to the repository.

10. C. To define the environment (development, production, etc.) and enable environment-specific configurations

Setting **NODE_ENV** allows the application to determine the current environment and load appropriate configurations or optimizations accordingly.

11. A. Hardcoding sensitive information directly into the code

Hardcoding sensitive data is insecure and should be avoided. Instead, use environment variables and secure storage methods.

12. B. It allows for conditional logging based on namespaces, reducing performance overhead when logs are disabled

The **debug** module enables logging messages to be conditionally output based on namespaces, and when not enabled, it incurs minimal performance overhead.

13. A. By setting the **DEBUG** environment variable to the desired namespace

You enable debug messages by setting the **DEBUG** environment variable to match the desired namespace(s) before running the application.

14. C. To handle exceptions that are not caught elsewhere and prevent the application from crashing abruptly

The **uncaughtException** event handler catches exceptions that weren't handled elsewhere, allowing you to log the error and perform cleanup before the application exits.

15. B. **parentPort**

Within a worker thread, **parentPort** is used to communicate with the parent thread by sending and receiving messages.

CHAPTER 4: NETWORK PROGRAMMING AND SECURITY

Overview

In this chapter, we'll look at the most important parts of network programming and security using Node.js. You'll learn how to build solid HTTP and HTTPS servers and clients, so your apps can communicate effectively over the internet. We'll look at how to handle requests and responses, manage routing, and put in place best practices for creating reliable server-client architectures that form the backbone of web services.

We'll also look at how to use TLS/SSL protocols to keep your communications secure. It's crucial to grasp how to set up encryption and create secure connections to keep data safe while building user trust. You'll get hands-on experience setting up SSL certificates and configuring your servers to use HTTPS. This will help you keep sensitive information confidential and secure during transmission. You'll also learn how to use UDP for quick, lightweight communication and how to do DNS lookups in your apps.

Finally, we'll look at building real-time apps with WebSockets and get to grips with HTTP/2 in Node.js. You'll learn how to use HTTP/2 to make your apps run faster with features like multiplexing and server push. Together, these topics give you the skills you need to develop secure, efficient, and modern network applications using Node.js.

Building Robust HTTP(S) Servers and Clients

We will begin with creating HTTP and HTTPS servers for our book publishing platform, handle requests and responses, and implement middleware to enhance functionality.

Setting up HTTP Server

Create a new directory for the project and initialize it:

```
mkdir book-platform
cd book-platform
npm init -y
```

We'll use Express.js to simplify server creation:

```
npm install express
```

Create an **app.js** file:

```
// file: app.js
const express = require('express');
```

```
const app = express();
// Middleware to parse JSON requests
app.use(express.json());
// Sample route
app.get('/', (req, res) => {
  res.send('Welcome to the Book Publishing Platform');
});
// Start the server
const PORT = process.env.PORT || 3000;
app.listen(PORT, () => {
  console.log(`Server is running on port ${PORT}`);
});
```

Start the server:

```
node app.js
```

Then finally, visit **http://localhost:3000/** in a browser to see the welcome message.

Handling Requests and Responses

First, we'll handle CRUD operations for books.

```
// file: routes/bookRoutes.js
const express = require('express');
const router = express.Router();
// In-memory data store
let books = [];
// Create a new book
router.post('/books', (req, res) => {
  const book = req.body;
  book.id = books.length + 1;
  books.push(book);
```

```
  res.status(201).json(book);
});
// Get all books
router.get('/books', (req, res) => {
  res.json(books);
});
// Get a book by ID
router.get('/books/:id', (req, res) => {
  const id = parseInt(req.params.id);
  const book = books.find((b) => b.id === id);
  if (book) {
    res.json(book);
  } else {
    res.status(404).json({ message: 'Book not found' });
  }
});
// Update a book by ID
router.put('/books/:id', (req, res) => {
  const id = parseInt(req.params.id);
  const index = books.findIndex((b) => b.id === id);
  if (index !== -1) {
    books[index] = { ...books[index], ...req.body };
    res.json(books[index]);
  } else {
    res.status(404).json({ message: 'Book not found' });
  }
});
// Delete a book by ID
router.delete('/books/:id', (req, res) => {
```

```
  const id = parseInt(req.params.id);
  const index = books.findIndex((b) => b.id === id);
  if (index !== -1) {
    const deletedBook = books.splice(index, 1);
    res.json(deletedBook);
  } else {
    res.status(404).json({ message: 'Book not found' });
  }
});
module.exports = router;
```

Next, update **app.js** to include the book routes:

```
// file: app.js
const express = require('express');
const app = express();
app.use(express.json());
const bookRoutes = require('./routes/bookRoutes');
app.use('/api', bookRoutes);
app.get('/', (req, res) => {
  res.send('Welcome to the Book Publishing Platform');
});
const PORT = process.env.PORT || 3000;
app.listen(PORT, () => {
  console.log(`Server is running on port ${PORT}`);
});
```

Then, make use of Postman or curl to test the API endpoints:

```
curl -X POST -H "Content-Type: application/json" -d
'{"title":"Node.js Basics","author":"John Doe"}'
http://localhost:3000/api/books
```

```
curl http://localhost:3000/api/books
curl http://localhost:3000/api/books/1
curl -X PUT -H "Content-Type: application/json" -d
'{"title":"Advanced Node.js"}'
http://localhost:3000/api/books/1
curl -X DELETE http://localhost:3000/api/books/1
```

Implementing Middleware

The middleware functions are the ones that can access the request and response objects and modify them or perform actions before passing control to the next middleware. To start with,

Create a middleware to log request details:

```
// file: middleware/logger.js
function logger(req, res, next) {
  console.log(`${req.method} ${req.url}`);
  next();
}
module.exports = logger;
```

Integrate it into **app.js**:

```
// file: app.js
const express = require('express');
const app = express();
const logger = require('./middleware/logger');
app.use(logger);
app.use(express.json());
const bookRoutes = require('./routes/bookRoutes');
app.use('/api', bookRoutes);
app.get('/', (req, res) => {
  res.send('Welcome to the Book Publishing Platform');
});
```

```
const PORT = process.env.PORT || 3000;
app.listen(PORT, () => {
  console.log(`Server is running on port ${PORT}`);
});
```

Now, every request will be logged to the console with its method and URL.

Error Handling Middleware

Create a middleware to handle errors:

```
// file: middleware/errorHandler.js
function errorHandler(err, req, res, next) {
  console.error(err.stack);
  res.status(500).json({ error: 'Something went wrong!' });
}
module.exports = errorHandler;
```

Integrate it at the end of the middleware stack in **app.js**:

```
// file: app.js
// ... previous code ...
const errorHandler = require('./middleware/errorHandler');
app.use(errorHandler);
// Start the server
const PORT = process.env.PORT || 3000;
app.listen(PORT, () => {
  console.log(`Server is running on port ${PORT}`);
});
```

Now, any errors thrown in the route handlers will be caught by this middleware.

Authentication Middleware

Suppose we want to protect certain routes.

```
// file: middleware/auth.js
function authenticate(req, res, next) {
  const token = req.headers['authorization'];
  if (token === 'secret-token') {
    next();
  } else {
    res.status(401).json({ message: 'Unauthorized' });
  }
}
module.exports = authenticate;
```

Apply this middleware to protected routes in **bookRoutes.js**:

```
// file: routes/bookRoutes.js
const express = require('express');
const router = express.Router();
const authenticate = require('../middleware/auth');
let books = [];
// Create a new book (protected route)
router.post('/books', authenticate, (req, res) => {
  const book = req.body;
  book.id = books.length + 1;
  books.push(book);
  res.status(201).json(book);
});
// Other routes remain the same
```

Now, to create a new book, the client must include the header **Authorization: secret-token**.

Upgrading to HTTPS

To secure communications, we'll set up an HTTPS server using self-signed certificates (for testing purposes).

Generate Self-Signed Certificates

Use OpenSSL to generate a key and certificate:

```
openssl genrsa -out key.pem 2048
openssl req -new -key key.pem -out csr.pem
openssl x509 -req -days 365 -in csr.pem -signkey key.pem -out
cert.pem
```

Fill in the required information when prompted.

Create HTTPS Server

Update **app.js**:

```
// file: app.js
const express = require('express');
const https = require('https');
const fs = require('fs');
const app = express();
// ... previous middleware and routes ...
// Read SSL certificate and key
const options = {
  key: fs.readFileSync('key.pem'),
  cert: fs.readFileSync('cert.pem'),
};
const PORT = process.env.PORT || 3000;
https.createServer(options, app).listen(PORT, () => {
  console.log(`HTTPS Server is running on port ${PORT}`);
});
```

Test the HTTPS Server

Start the server:

```
node app.js
```

Access **https://localhost:3000/** in a browser. You may need to accept the self-signed certificate warning.

Redirect HTTP to HTTPS

To ensure all traffic uses HTTPS, set up a redirect from HTTP to HTTPS.

```
// file: app.js
const express = require('express');
const https = require('https');
const http = require('http');
const fs = require('fs');
const app = express();
// ... previous middleware and routes ...
// HTTPS server options
const options = {
  key: fs.readFileSync('key.pem'),
  cert: fs.readFileSync('cert.pem'),
};
const HTTPS_PORT = process.env.HTTPS_PORT || 3000;
const HTTP_PORT = process.env.HTTP_PORT || 80;
// HTTPS Server
https.createServer(options, app).listen(HTTPS_PORT, () => {
  console.log(`HTTPS Server is running on port
${HTTPS_PORT}`);
});
// HTTP Server for redirect
const httpApp = express();
httpApp.get('*', (req, res) => {
  res.redirect(`https://${req.headers.host}${req.url}`);
});
http.createServer(httpApp).listen(HTTP_PORT, () => {
```

```
  console.log(`HTTP Server is running on port ${HTTP_PORT} and
redirecting to HTTPS`);
});
```

If behind a proxy or load balancer, you might need to force HTTPS in Express.

```
// file: middleware/forceHttps.js
function forceHttps(req, res, next) {
  if (req.secure || req.headers['x-forwarded-proto'] ===
'https') {
    return next();
  }
  res.redirect(`https://${req.headers.host}${req.url}`);
}
module.exports = forceHttps;
```

Apply it in **app.js**:

```
// file: app.js
const forceHttps = require('./middleware/forceHttps');
app.use(forceHttps);
// ... rest of the code ...
```

Implementing Static File Serving

You can serve static files like images, CSS, and JavaScript files. To get started, just create a public directory and add some static files to it.

Use Express Static Middleware

```
// file: app.js
app.use(express.static('public'));
// Now, files in the public directory are accessible via
'/filename'
```

Adding a Template Engine

To render dynamic HTML pages.

Install EJS

```
npm install ejs
```

Setup EJS in Express

```
// file: app.js
app.set('view engine', 'ejs');
```

Create a View

Create a directory **views** and add **index.ejs**:

```
<!-- file: views/index.ejs -->
<!DOCTYPE html>
<html>
<head>
  <title>Book Publishing Platform</title>
</head>
<body>
  <h1>Welcome to the Book Publishing Platform</h1>
</body>
</html>
```

Render the View

Update the root route:

```
// file: app.js
app.get('/', (req, res) => {
  res.render('index');
});
```

Implementing Body Parsing Middleware

For handling form submissions and URL-encoded data, we recommend using Express' built-in middleware.

```
// file: app.js
app.use(express.urlencoded({ extended: true }));
```

Then, create a route to handle form submissions:

```
// file: routes/formRoutes.js
const express = require('express');
const router = express.Router();
router.post('/submit', (req, res) => {
  const formData = req.body;
  res.json({ message: 'Form submitted', data: formData });
});
module.exports = router;
```

Integrate into **app.js:**

```
// file: app.js
const formRoutes = require('./routes/formRoutes');
app.use('/api', formRoutes);
```

By following these steps, we've built a robust HTTP/HTTPS server for our book publishing platform. We've handled requests and responses, implemented middleware for logging, error handling, and authentication, and added features like static file serving and template rendering.

Implementing TLS/SSL for Secure Communications

We're going to beef up the security of our book publishing platform by adding TLS/SSL protocols to our existing server. We'll also make sure that the data transfer between clients and servers is encrypted.

Obtaining SSL/TLS Certificates

For secure communication, we need SSL/TLS certificates. In a production environment, you should obtain certificates from a trusted Certificate Authority (CA). For testing purposes, we'll generate self-signed certificates.

Generate a Private Key and Certificate

Open a terminal in the project directory and run:

```
# Generate a private key
openssl genrsa -out server.key 2048
# Generate a Certificate Signing Request (CSR)
openssl req -new -key server.key -out server.csr
```

When prompted, enter information such as Country Name, State, etc. For Common Name, use **localhost** if testing locally.

Create the Self-Signed Certificate

```
openssl x509 -req -days 365 -in server.csr -signkey server.key
-out server.crt
```

We now have **server.key** (private key) and **server.crt** (certificate).

Integrating TLS/SSL into the Server

Update Dependencies

Ensure you have the required modules:

```
npm install express
```

Modify the Server Code

Update **app.js** to create an HTTPS server using the certificates.

```
// file: app.js
const express = require('express');
const https = require('https');
const http = require('http');
const fs = require('fs');
const path = require('path');
const app = express();
// Middleware
```

```
app.use(express.json());
// Routes
const bookRoutes = require('./routes/bookRoutes');
app.use('/api', bookRoutes);
app.get('/', (req, res) => {
  res.send('Welcome to the Secure Book Publishing Platform');
});
// SSL options
const sslOptions = {
  key: fs.readFileSync(path.join(__dirname, 'server.key')),
  cert: fs.readFileSync(path.join(__dirname, 'server.crt')),
};
const HTTPS_PORT = process.env.HTTPS_PORT || 3000;
const HTTP_PORT = process.env.HTTP_PORT || 80;
// HTTPS Server
https.createServer(sslOptions, app).listen(HTTPS_PORT, () => {
  console.log(`HTTPS Server is running on port
${HTTPS_PORT}`);
});
// Redirect HTTP to HTTPS
const httpApp = express();
httpApp.get('*', (req, res) => {
  res.redirect(`https://${req.headers.host}${req.url}`);
});
http.createServer(httpApp).listen(HTTP_PORT, () => {
  console.log(`HTTP Server is running on port ${HTTP_PORT} and
redirecting to HTTPS`);
});
```

Here, it's important to keep your certificates secure. You can do this by putting the **server.key** and **server.crt** files in a safe place. Also, make sure to update the paths in **sslOptions**.

Verifying Encrypted Data Transmission

To confirm that the data transmission is encrypted, we'll use two methods:

Using OpenSSL's 's_client'

OpenSSL can test the SSL connection and display the certificate.

```
openssl s_client -connect localhost:3000
```

Using Wireshark to Inspect Traffic

First, install Wireshark from its official download page. You can open Wireshark and start capturing traffic on the loopback interface.

Then, apply the filter **tcp.port == 3000** to isolate the relevant traffic. A browser will allow you to visit **https://localhost:3000/**. The captured packets will include TLS traffic with encrypted payloads. You will not see plain text requests or responses, unlike HTTP. This lack of plain text data confirms that the transmission is encrypted.

Testing Application Functionality

Ensure that all routes and functionalities work over HTTPS.

For this, use **curl** with the **-k** flag to bypass certificate validation (for self-signed certificates):

Create a Book:

```
curl -k -X POST -H "Content-Type: application/json" -d
'{"title":"Secure Node.js","author":"Jane Doe"}'
https://localhost:3000/api/books
```

Get All Books:

```
curl -k https://localhost:3000/api/books
```

Now, test the Authentication Middleware

Unauthorized Access:

```
curl -k -X POST -H "Content-Type: application/json" -d
'{"title":"Unauthorized Access"}'
https://localhost:3000/api/books
```

You should receive a 401 Unauthorized response.

Authorized Access:

```
curl -k -X POST -H "Content-Type: application/json" -H
"Authorization: secret-token" -d '{"title":"Authorized
Access","author":"Alice"}' https://localhost:3000/api/books
```

Here, you should now be able to successfully create a new book.

Enforcing Secure Communication

To ensure all communication uses HTTPS, we need to handle cases where clients might try to access the server via HTTP.

Force HTTPS Middleware

If using a proxy or load balancer (e.g., in production), implement middleware to redirect or reject HTTP requests.

```
// file: middleware/forceHttps.js
function forceHttps(req, res, next) {
  if (req.secure || req.headers['x-forwarded-proto'] ===
'https') {
    return next();
  }
  res.redirect(`https://${req.headers.host}${req.url}`);
}
module.exports = forceHttps;
```

Integrate Middleware

```
// file: app.js
const forceHttps = require('./middleware/forceHttps');
app.use(forceHttps);
```

Configuring for Production

If you're working in a production environment, it's best to use certificates from a trusted CA. You can get certificates from services like Let's Encrypt, which offer free SSL certificates. Just follow their instructions to generate certificates for your domain.

Update SSL Options

Replace the self-signed certificate paths with the paths to your trusted certificates.

```
const sslOptions = {
  key: fs.readFileSync('/path/to/your/privkey.pem'),
  cert: fs.readFileSync('/path/to/your/fullchain.pem'),
};
```

Security Enhancements

First, disable insecure protocols and ciphers:

```
const sslOptions = {
  // ... previous options
  secureProtocol: 'TLSv1_2_method',
  ciphers: 'ECDHE-RSA-AES256-GCM-
SHA384:...:!aNULL:!eNULL:!MD5',
  honorCipherOrder: true,
};
```

You can set the HTTP security headers using the helmet middleware.

```
npm install helmet
```

Integrate it into **app.js**:

```
const helmet = require('helmet');
app.use(helmet());
```

By adding TLS/SSL protocols to our server, we've made it harder for people to intercept the messages going back and forth between clients and our servers. We've checked that the data is encrypted using OpenSSL and Wireshark. When we're in production, we always use certificates that come from a company we trust, and we regularly check our SSL configuration to make sure there are no holes in it.

Working with UDP and DNS Modules

Introduction to UDP Datagram Sockets

In this topic, we'll look at how to use UDP datagram sockets and DNS modules in Node.js. We'll show you how to send and receive messages using UDP and how to resolve domain names using the DNS module in our book publishing platform. While our platform mainly uses HTTP/HTTPS protocols, it's good to understand UDP and DNS so you can add features like real-time notifications or custom network services.

UDP (User Datagram Protocol) is a connectionless protocol that allows sending messages (datagrams) without establishing a connection. It's faster and has lower overhead compared to TCP but doesn't guarantee delivery, order, or error checking. UDP is suitable for applications where speed is critical, and occasional data loss is acceptable.

Node.js has this thing called the **dgram** module that you can use to work with UDP sockets.

Creating UDP Server and Client

First, we'll create a simple UDP server and client to send and receive messages.

UDP Server

Create a file named **udpServer.js**:

```
// file: udpServer.js
const dgram = require('dgram');
const server = dgram.createSocket('udp4');
const PORT = 41234;
server.on('error', (err) => {
  console.error(`Server error:\n${err.stack}`);
  server.close();
});
server.on('message', (msg, rinfo) => {
  console.log(`Server got message: ${msg} from
${rinfo.address}:${rinfo.port}`);
  // Echo the message back to the client
  const response = Buffer.from(`Received: ${msg}`);
  server.send(response, rinfo.port, rinfo.address, (err) => {
    if (err) {
```

```
      console.error(`Error sending response: ${err}`);
    } else {
      console.log(`Sent response to
${rinfo.address}:${rinfo.port}`);
    }
  });
});
server.on('listening', () => {
  const address = server.address();
  console.log(`UDP server listening on
${address.address}:${address.port}`);
});
server.bind(PORT);
```

Here, in the aboove program,

We import the **dgram** module and create a UDP socket using **udp4** (IPv4).
We handle the **error**, **message**, and **listening** events.
When a message is received, we log it and send a response back to the client.

UDP Client

Create a file named **udpClient.js**:

```
// file: udpClient.js
const dgram = require('dgram');
const client = dgram.createSocket('udp4');
const message = Buffer.from('Hello UDP Server');
const PORT = 41234;
const HOST = 'localhost';
client.send(message, PORT, HOST, (err) => {
  if (err) {
    console.error(`Client error: ${err}`);
    client.close();
```

```
  } else {
    console.log(`Message sent to ${HOST}:${PORT}`);
  }
});
client.on('message', (msg, rinfo) => {
  console.log(`Client received: ${msg} from
${rinfo.address}:${rinfo.port}`);
  client.close();
});
```

We'll start by creating a UDP client socket. We send a message to the server, and then we handle the message event to receive the response from the server.

Running UDP Server and Client

Start the UDP server:

```
node udpServer.js
```

In another terminal, run the UDP client:

```
node udpClient.js
```

Following is the server output:

```
UDP server listening on 0.0.0.0:41234
Server got message: Hello UDP Server from 127.0.0.1:XXXXX
Sent response to 127.0.0.1:XXXXX
```

And this given below is the client output:

```
Message sent to localhost:41234
Client received: Received: Hello UDP Server from
127.0.0.1:41234
```

Integrating UDP

Suppose we want to implement a feature where the server can broadcast notifications (e.g., new book releases) to multiple clients using UDP.

UDP Notification Server

Let us first modify **udpServer.js** to broadcast messages:

```
// file: udpNotificationServer.js
const dgram = require('dgram');
const server = dgram.createSocket('udp4');
const PORT = 41234;
const BROADCAST_ADDR = '255.255.255.255';
server.bind(() => {
  server.setBroadcast(true);
});
function sendNotification(message) {
  const msgBuffer = Buffer.from(message);
  server.send(msgBuffer, 0, msgBuffer.length, PORT,
BROADCAST_ADDR, (err) => {
    if (err) {
      console.error(`Broadcast error: ${err}`);
    } else {
      console.log(`Broadcasted message: ${message}`);
    }
  });
}
// Send a notification every 5 seconds
setInterval(() => {
  sendNotification('New book released!');
}, 5000);
```

UDP Notification Client

Create **udpNotificationClient.js**:

```
// file: udpNotificationClient.js
```

```
const dgram = require('dgram');
const client = dgram.createSocket('udp4');
const PORT = 41234;
client.on('listening', () => {
  const address = client.address();
  console.log(`UDP client listening on
${address.address}:${address.port}`);
});
client.on('message', (msg, rinfo) => {
  console.log(`Notification received: ${msg} from
${rinfo.address}:${rinfo.port}`);
});
client.bind(PORT);
```

Running Notification Server and Client

For this, start the notification client on multiple terminals or machines:

```
node udpNotificationClient.js
```

Then, start the notification server:

```
node udpNotificationServer.js
```

The server broadcasts messages to all clients listening on the specified port. Clients then receive notifications without establishing a connection.

Introduction to DNS Module

The **dns** module in Node.js provides functions for performing DNS queries, such as resolving domain names to IP addresses.

Here, we'll demonstrate how to resolve domain names using the **dns** module.

Basic DNS Lookup

First, create a file named **dnsLookup.js**:

```
// file: dnsLookup.js
```

```
const dns = require('dns');
const domain = 'example.com';
dns.lookup(domain, (err, address, family) => {
  if (err) {
    console.error(`DNS lookup error: ${err}`);
  } else {
    console.log(`Address: ${address}, Family: IPv${family}`);
  }
});
```

Run the script:

```
node dnsLookup.js
```

Following is the expected output:

```
Address: 93.184.216.34, Family: IPv4
```

Resolving with 'dns.resolve'

The **dns.resolve** method can retrieve different DNS records.

```
// file: dnsResolve.js
const dns = require('dns');
const domain = 'example.com';
dns.resolve(domain, 'A', (err, addresses) => {
  if (err) {
    console.error(`DNS resolve error: ${err}`);
  } else {
    console.log(`A records: ${addresses}`);
  }
});
```

Reverse DNS Lookup

Perform a reverse lookup to find the domain associated with an IP address.

```
// file: dnsReverse.js
const dns = require('dns');
const ip = '8.8.8.8';
dns.reverse(ip, (err, hostnames) => {
  if (err) {
    console.error(`Reverse lookup error: ${err}`);
  } else {
    console.log(`Hostnames for IP ${ip}: ${hostnames}`);
  }
});
```

Integrating DNS into App

In our Express application, add a route to resolve domain names. For this, edit the **app.js** or create a new route file:

```
// file: routes/dnsRoutes.js
const express = require('express');
const dns = require('dns');
const router = express.Router();
router.get('/resolve', (req, res) => {
  const domain = req.query.domain;
  if (!domain) {
    return res.status(400).json({ error: 'Domain parameter is
required' });
  }
  dns.lookup(domain, (err, address, family) => {
    if (err) {
      return res.status(500).json({ error: `DNS lookup error:
${err.message}` });
    }
```

```
    res.json({ domain, address, family: `IPv${family}` });
  });
});
module.exports = router;
```

Integrate the route into **app.js**:

```
const dnsRoutes = require('./routes/dnsRoutes');
app.use('/api', dnsRoutes);
```

Start the server and access the route:

```
curl "http://localhost:3000/api/resolve?domain=example.com"
```

Following is the possible output:

```
{
  "domain": "example.com",
  "address": "93.184.216.34",
  "family": "IPv4"
}
```

Using Promises with DNS Module

The **dns** module also provides promise-based methods in Node.js v10 and above. Following is a quick example of **dns.promises**:

```
// file: dnsPromises.js
const dns = require('dns').promises;
async function resolveDomain(domain) {
  try {
    const addresses = await dns.resolve4(domain);
    console.log(`Addresses: ${addresses.join(', ')}`);
  } catch (err) {
    console.error(`Error: ${err}`);
```

```
    }
}
resolveDomain('example.com');
```

By working with the UDP and DNS modules in Node.js, we've learned how to send and receive messages using UDP datagram sockets and how to resolve domain names within our application. While our book publishing platform may not use UDP extensively, understanding these modules expands our ability to handle various networking tasks, implement real-time features, or integrate with lower-level network services.

Using WebSockets

Introduction to WebSockets

WebSockets provide a persistent, bi-directional communication channel between the client and server over a single TCP connection. Unlike HTTP, which follows a request-response model, WebSockets allow servers to push data to clients in real-time without the need for clients to poll the server periodically.

Here are some of the advantages of using WebSockets in our application:

Users get instant notifications about new books or updates without having to refresh the page.
Real-time features make the user experience better by keeping users engaged with timely information.
WebSockets cut down on the need for constant polling, which saves bandwidth and eases the load on servers.

Here are some examples of how our platform can be used:

- Add a customer support chat feature using WebSockets.
- Real-time analytics are also a great feature.
- Let authors know how their books are selling or how many views they're getting in real time.
- Let multiple users work on a manuscript together in real time.

Implementing WebSockets

Now, we'll enhance our existing Express.js application by adding WebSocket functionality. We'll use the **ws** library, a simple WebSocket implementation for Node.js.

First, install the **ws** library:

```
npm install ws
```

We'll then update our **app.js** to integrate WebSockets.

```
// file: app.js
const express = require('express');
const https = require('https');
const fs = require('fs');
const path = require('path');
const WebSocket = require('ws'); // Import the ws library
const app = express();
// Middleware
app.use(express.json());
// Routes
const bookRoutes = require('./routes/bookRoutes');
app.use('/api', bookRoutes);
app.get('/', (req, res) => {
  res.sendFile(path.join(__dirname, 'views', 'index.html'));
});
// SSL options
const sslOptions = {
  key: fs.readFileSync(path.join(__dirname, 'server.key')),
  cert: fs.readFileSync(path.join(__dirname, 'server.crt')),
};
const HTTPS_PORT = process.env.HTTPS_PORT || 3000;
// Create HTTPS server
const server = https.createServer(sslOptions, app);
// Create WebSocket server
const wss = new WebSocket.Server({ server });
// Broadcast function to send data to all connected clients
```

```
wss.broadcast = function (data) {
  wss.clients.forEach(function (client) {
    if (client.readyState === WebSocket.OPEN) {
      client.send(data);
    }
  });
};
// Handle WebSocket connections
wss.on('connection', (ws) => {
  console.log('Client connected via WebSocket');
  ws.on('message', (message) => {
    console.log(`Received message from client: ${message}`);
    // Handle messages from clients if needed
  });
  ws.on('close', () => {
    console.log('Client disconnected');
  });
});
// Start the server
server.listen(HTTPS_PORT, () => {
  console.log(`HTTPS Server is running on port
${HTTPS_PORT}`);
});
```

In the above script,

- We import the **ws** library and create a WebSocket server (**wss**) that attaches to our HTTPS server.
- We define a **broadcast** function to send messages to all connected WebSocket clients.
- We handle **connection**, **message**, and **close** events for WebSocket clients.

Then, we modify **bookRoutes.js** to broadcast updates when books are added or modified.

```
// file: routes/bookRoutes.js
const express = require('express');
const router = express.Router();
const authenticate = require('../middleware/auth');
// In-memory data store
let books = [];
// Reference to WebSocket server
let wss = null;
// Function to set WebSocket server instance
function setWebSocketServer(server) {
  wss = server;
}
// Create a new book (protected route)
router.post('/books', authenticate, (req, res) => {
  const book = req.body;
  book.id = books.length + 1;
  books.push(book);
  res.status(201).json(book);
  // Notify connected clients about the new book
  if (wss) {
    const data = JSON.stringify({ event: 'newBook', book });
    wss.broadcast(data);
  }
});
// Update a book by ID (protected route)
router.put('/books/:id', authenticate, (req, res) => {
  const id = parseInt(req.params.id);
  const index = books.findIndex((b) => b.id === id);
  if (index !== -1) {
```

```
    books[index] = { ...books[index], ...req.body };
    res.json(books[index]);
    // Notify connected clients about the updated book
    if (wss) {
      const data = JSON.stringify({ event: 'updateBook', book:
books[index] });
      wss.broadcast(data);
    }
  } else {
    res.status(404).json({ message: 'Book not found' });
  }
});
// Other routes remain the same
module.exports = { router, setWebSocketServer };
```

Here,

- We add a **setWebSocketServer** function to pass the WebSocket server instance to the routes.
- After adding or updating a book, we broadcast a message to all connected clients with the event type and book data.

We then update **app.js** to Pass WebSocket Server to Routes

```
// After creating wss
const { router: bookRoutes, setWebSocketServer } =
require('./routes/bookRoutes');
app.use('/api', bookRoutes);
// Set the WebSocket server in routes
setWebSocketServer(wss);
```

Next, we'll update **index.html** to establish a WebSocket connection and handle incoming messages.

```
<!-- file: views/index.html -->
<!DOCTYPE html>
```

```
<html>
<head>
  <title>Book Publishing Platform</title>
</head>
<body>
  <h1>Welcome to the Book Publishing Platform</h1>
  <div id="books">
    <!-- Books will be displayed here -->
  </div>
  <script>
    // Establish WebSocket connection
    const protocol = window.location.protocol === 'https:' ?
'wss' : 'ws';
    const socket = new
WebSocket(`${protocol}://${window.location.host}`);
    socket.addEventListener('open', () => {
      console.log('Connected to WebSocket server');
    });
    socket.addEventListener('message', (event) => {
      const data = JSON.parse(event.data);
      if (data.event === 'newBook') {
        addBookToPage(data.book);
        alert(`New book added: ${data.book.title}`);
      } else if (data.event === 'updateBook') {
        updateBookOnPage(data.book);
        alert(`Book updated: ${data.book.title}`);
      }
    });
    socket.addEventListener('close', () => {
      console.log('Disconnected from WebSocket server');
```

```
    });
    // Function to fetch and display books
    function fetchBooks() {
      fetch('/api/books')
        .then(response => response.json())
        .then(books => {
          const booksDiv = document.getElementById('books');
          booksDiv.innerHTML = '';
          books.forEach(addBookToPage);
        })
        .catch(error => console.error('Error fetching books:',
error));
    }
    function addBookToPage(book) {
      const booksDiv = document.getElementById('books');
      const bookDiv = document.createElement('div');
      bookDiv.id = `book-${book.id}`;
      bookDiv.textContent = `ID: ${book.id}, Title:
${book.title}, Author: ${book.author}`;
      booksDiv.appendChild(bookDiv);
    }
    function updateBookOnPage(book) {
      const bookDiv = document.getElementById(`book-
${book.id}`);
      if (bookDiv) {
        bookDiv.textContent = `ID: ${book.id}, Title:
${book.title}, Author: ${book.author}`;
      } else {
        addBookToPage(book);
      }
```

```
    }
    // Fetch books on page load
    fetchBooks();
  </script>
</body>
</html>
```

In the above script,

- We establish a WebSocket connection to the server.
- We listen for messages (**'message'** event) and handle different event types (**'newBook'**, **'updateBook'**).
- We update the DOM to display the list of books and reflect real-time changes.

Then make a use of **curl** to send a POST request:

```
curl -k -X POST -H "Content-Type: application/json" -H
"Authorization: secret-token" -d '{"title":"Real-Time
Node.js","author":"Eve"}' https://localhost:3000/api/books
```

Next, we display notifications, for which, instead of using **alert()**, we implement a more user-friendly notification system.

```
<!-- Add to index.html -->
<style>
  #notification {
    position: fixed;
    top: 10px;
    right: 10px;
    background: #f0ad4e;
    color: white;
    padding: 10px;
    border-radius: 5px;
    display: none;
  }
</style>
```

```
<div id="notification"></div>
<script>
  // Function to show notifications
  function showNotification(message) {
    const notificationDiv =
document.getElementById('notification');
    notificationDiv.textContent = message;
    notificationDiv.style.display = 'block';
    setTimeout(() => {
      notificationDiv.style.display = 'none';
    }, 3000);
  }
  // Replace alert() with showNotification()
  socket.addEventListener('message', (event) => {
    const data = JSON.parse(event.data);
    if (data.event === 'newBook') {
      addBookToPage(data.book);
      showNotification(`New book added: ${data.book.title}`);
    } else if (data.event === 'updateBook') {
      updateBookOnPage(data.book);
      showNotification(`Book updated: ${data.book.title}`);
    }
  });
</script>
```

Then, implement reconnection logic if the WebSocket connection is lost.

```
// Modify the WebSocket connection code
function connectWebSocket() {
  const protocol = window.location.protocol === 'https:' ?
'wss' : 'ws';
```

```
  const socket = new
WebSocket(`${protocol}://${window.location.host}`);
  socket.addEventListener('open', () => {
    console.log('Connected to WebSocket server');
  });
  socket.addEventListener('message', (event) => {
    // Handle messages
  });
  socket.addEventListener('close', () => {
    console.log('Disconnected from WebSocket server.
Reconnecting in 5 seconds...');
    setTimeout(connectWebSocket, 5000);
  });
}
// Initialize WebSocket connection
connectWebSocket();
```

Securing WebSocket Communications

Because we're using HTTPS, our WebSocket connections (WSS) are encrypted. Just make sure that any sensitive data sent over WebSockets is properly secured.

Authentication

First, implement authentication for WebSocket connections if needed.

```
// Client-side
const socket = new
WebSocket(`${protocol}://${window.location.host}?token=your_to
ken`);
// Server-side
wss.on('connection', (ws, request) => {
  const params = new
URLSearchParams(request.url.split('?')[1]);
```

```
  const token = params.get('token');
  // Validate token
});
```

Note that custom headers are not supported in WebSocket connections initiated from browsers.

Handling Origin Verification

Verify the origin of the connection to prevent cross-site WebSocket hijacking.

```
wss.on('connection', (ws, request) => {
  const origin = request.headers.origin;
  if (origin !== 'https://yourdomain.com') {
    ws.close();
    return;
  }
  // Proceed with connection
});
```

Scaling WebSocket Connections

In a production environment, you might need to handle a lot of WebSocket connections and make sure you can grow as your company grows. A good option for publishing and subscribing to events across multiple server instances is a message broker like Redis. You'll probably also want to make sure your WebSocket connections are properly load-balanced, which might involve using sticky sessions.

Next, implement proper error handling to improve reliability.

```
wss.on('error', (error) => {
  console.error('WebSocket server error:', error);
});
ws.on('error', (error) => {
  console.error('WebSocket client error:', error);
});
```

By using WebSockets, we've made our book publishing platform more responsive by adding instant data updates. If you're connected to the server, you'll get a heads-up when new books are added or existing books are updated in real time.

Summary

In a nutshell, we covered a lot of ground on network programming and security for Node.js. We started off by setting up HTTP and HTTPS servers with Express.js, and learned how to handle requests and responses effectively. Next, we looked at how to use TLS/SSL protocols to keep our server communications safe and secure. This meant setting up SSL options in our server code and checking the encryption using tools like OpenSSL and Wireshark.

Next, we moved on to working with UDP datagram sockets and the DNS module. We set up UDP servers and clients to send and receive messages, and we figured out when UDP's connectionless communication is a good fit. We also used the DNS module to resolve domain names within our application. This lets us translate domain names to IP addresses and vice versa. Finally, we added WebSockets to our app so we could send real-time updates to users. This meant we could let them know when new books were added or existing ones were updated.

Throughout the chapter, we used real-world examples to help us understand Node.js concepts. By building and modifying our sample app, we learned how to create secure and efficient network communications, which are essential for modern web development.

Knowledge Exercise

1. Which Node.js module is commonly used to create an HTTP server that can handle routing and middleware?

A. **http**

B. **express**

C. **net**

D. **ws**

2. When setting up an HTTPS server in Node.js, which two key components are required for SSL/TLS encryption?

A. Private key and certificate

B. Username and password

C. API key and secret

D. Domain name and IP address

3. In the context of securing a Node.js server with TLS/SSL, what is the purpose of a self-signed certificate?

A. It authenticates the server with a trusted authority

B. It encrypts data for testing purposes without third-party validation

C. It provides a certificate that never expires

D. It enhances performance by skipping encryption

4. Which Node.js module is used to create UDP datagram sockets for sending and receiving messages?

A. **dgram**

B. **dns**

C. **net**

D. **socket.io**

5. What is a primary characteristic of UDP compared to TCP in network communications?

A. UDP guarantees delivery and order of messages

B. UDP is connection-oriented and reliable

C. UDP is faster but does not guarantee delivery

D. UDP requires a handshake before data transmission

6. How can you perform a DNS lookup to resolve a domain name to an IP address in Node.js?

A. By using the **net** module's **lookup()** function

B. By using the **dns** module's **lookup()** function

C. By sending an HTTP request to a DNS server

D. By reading the **/etc/hosts** file directly

7. In Node.js, which method is used to create a WebSocket server using the **ws** library?

A. **new ws.Server()**

B. **ws.createServer()**

C. **http.createWebSocketServer()**

D. **express.websocket()**

8. What advantage do WebSockets have over traditional HTTP polling methods?

A. They use less secure protocols

B. They allow persistent bi-directional communication

C. They increase server load due to constant connections

D. They require more bandwidth for the same data

9. When a WebSocket connection is established, which protocol upgrade header is used in the initial HTTP request?

A. **Upgrade: TCP**

B. **Upgrade: UDP**

C. **Upgrade: websocket**

D. **Upgrade: tls**

10. In implementing WebSockets with the **ws** library, how do you broadcast a message to all connected clients?

A. Loop through **wss.clients** and send the message to each client

B. Use **wss.broadcast()** method directly

C. Send the message to a specific client ID

D. Use **wss.sendToAll()** method

11. Which of the following is a limitation of using self-signed certificates in a production environment?

A. They are not compatible with HTTPS

B. Browsers will not trust them without warnings

C. They provide stronger encryption than CA-signed certificates

D. They are more expensive than certificates from trusted authorities

12. What is the main purpose of using middleware in an Express.js application?

A. To serve static files only

B. To handle low-level networking tasks

C. To execute functions that have access to the request and response objects and can modify them

D. To compile and bundle front-end assets

13. In a UDP communication setup, what happens if packets are lost during transmission?

A. The protocol automatically requests retransmission

B. The packets are re-sent by default

C. The data is lost, and the application must handle it

D. The connection is closed immediately

14. Which method from the **dns** module can be used to perform a reverse DNS lookup?

A. **dns.lookupService()**

B. **dns.reverse()**

C. **dns.resolvePtr()**

D. **dns.getServers()**

15. What is the main benefit of integrating WebSockets into a Node.js application?

A. Improved SEO performance

B. Ability to handle file uploads efficiently

C. Real-time communication between client and server

D. Simplified handling of HTTP POST requests

Answers and Explanations

1. B. **express**

Express.js is a web application framework for Node.js that simplifies the creation of HTTP servers, handling routing and middleware efficiently.

2. A. Private key and certificate

An HTTPS server requires a private key and a certificate to establish encrypted communications using SSL/TLS protocols.

3. B. It encrypts data for testing purposes without third-party validation

A self-signed certificate allows for encryption but is not trusted by browsers as it isn't signed by a recognized Certificate Authority, making it suitable for testing.

4. A. **dgram**

The **dgram** module provides an implementation of UDP datagram sockets for sending and receiving messages.

5. C. UDP is faster but does not guarantee delivery

UDP is a connectionless protocol that is faster due to lower overhead but does not guarantee message delivery or order.

6. B. By using the **dns** module's **lookup()** function

The **dns.lookup()** function from the **dns** module resolves a domain name to an IP address.

7. A. **new ws.Server()**

Creating a new WebSocket server with the **ws** library involves instantiating **ws.Server()**.

8. B. They allow persistent bi-directional communication

WebSockets enable a continuous connection allowing real-time data exchange between client and server without the need for repeated HTTP requests.

9. C. **Upgrade: websocket**

The **Upgrade: websocket** header in the initial HTTP request signals the server to switch the protocol to WebSocket.

10. A. Loop through **wss.clients** and send the message to each client

To broadcast a message, iterate over **wss.clients** and send the message to each connected client.

11. B. Browsers will not trust them without warnings

Self-signed certificates are not trusted by browsers, resulting in security warnings, which is unacceptable for production environments.

12. C. To execute functions that have access to the request and response objects and can modify them

Middleware functions in Express.js can process requests and responses, modify them, or end the request-response cycle.

13. C. The data is lost, and the application must handle it

UDP does not provide mechanisms for retransmission; lost packets are not recovered unless handled by the application layer.

14. B. **dns.reverse()**

The **dns.reverse()** method performs a reverse DNS lookup, resolving an IP address to a domain name.

15. C. Real-time communication between client and server

Integrating WebSockets allows for real-time, two-way communication, enabling instant data updates in applications.

CHAPTER 5: FILE SYSTEMS AND DATA STREAMS

Overview

In this chapter, we will master the advanced aspects of working with file systems and data streams in Node.js. You will learn how to perform sophisticated file system operations, including handling file permissions, monitoring file system changes, and efficiently manipulating directories and files. We will also master streams for efficient data processing. You can handle large amounts of data without overwhelming system memory by understanding how to work with readable, writable, duplex, and transform streams.

You will learn how to pipe streams together, manage backpressure, and handle stream events effectively. We will cover the creation of custom stream implementations. You can tailor data processing to your application's specific needs by designing your own streams. This provides more control over how data is read, transformed, and written. You will learn how to build custom transform streams to apply complex data transformations on the fly, enhancing the flexibility and efficiency of your data processing tasks.

Furthermore, we will discuss how to manage large data sets with buffers and integrate the crypto module for data security. You will learn how to work with binary data using buffers, which is vital for handling files, network packets, or any binary protocols. You will also learn how to integrate the crypto module to encrypt and decrypt data, create hashes, and ensure data integrity and security within your applications.

Advanced File System Operations

In this section, we'll explore advanced file system operations in Node.js by handling asynchronous file operations, implementing file watching, and managing file permissions within our book publishing platform. These techniques are crucial for building applications that interact efficiently with the file system, especially when dealing with user-uploaded files, generating reports, or monitoring changes in files and directories.

Handling Asynchronous File Operations

The Node.js **fs** module is the way to interact with the file system. We will focus on asynchronous methods to prevent blocking the event loop.

Let's look at an example of reading and writing files asynchronously. Here, suppose that we want to store user-uploaded book manuscripts and read them when needed.

- Writing File Asynchronously

```
// file: controllers/fileController.js
const fs = require('fs');
const path = require('path');
```

```
// Function to save a manuscript
function saveManuscript(fileName, content) {
  const filePath = path.join(__dirname, 'manuscripts',
fileName);
  fs.writeFile(filePath, content, 'utf8', (err) => {
    if (err) {
      console.error(`Error saving manuscript:
${err.message}`);
    } else {
      console.log(`Manuscript ${fileName} saved
successfully.`);
    }
  });
}
module.exports = {
  saveManuscript,
};
```

Here, we used **fs.writeFile()** to write data to a file asynchronously. It handles errors and confirms successful writing.

- Reading File Asynchronously

```
// file: controllers/fileController.js
// Function to read a manuscript
function readManuscript(fileName, callback) {
  const filePath = path.join(__dirname, 'manuscripts',
fileName);
  fs.readFile(filePath, 'utf8', (err, data) => {
    if (err) {
      console.error(`Error reading manuscript:
${err.message}`);
      callback(err);
```

```
    } else {
      console.log(`Manuscript ${fileName} read
successfully.`);
      callback(null, data);
    }
  });
}
module.exports = {
  saveManuscript,
  readManuscript,
};
```

- Using Functions in Routes

```
// file: routes/manuscriptRoutes.js
const express = require('express');
const router = express.Router();
const { saveManuscript, readManuscript } =
require('../controllers/fileController');
// Route to upload a manuscript
router.post('/manuscripts', (req, res) => {
  const { fileName, content } = req.body;
  saveManuscript(fileName, content);
  res.status(201).json({ message: 'Manuscript uploaded
successfully.' });
});
// Route to get a manuscript
router.get('/manuscripts/:fileName', (req, res) => {
  const fileName = req.params.fileName;
  readManuscript(fileName, (err, data) => {
    if (err) {
```

```
      res.status(500).json({ error: 'Failed to read
manuscript.' });
    } else {
      res.send(data);
    }
  });
});
module.exports = router;
```

For better readability and error handling, we can use promises with **fs.promises**.

```
// file: controllers/fileController.js
const fs = require('fs').promises;
const path = require('path');
// Function to save a manuscript using promises
async function saveManuscript(fileName, content) {
  const filePath = path.join(__dirname, 'manuscripts',
fileName);
  try {
    await fs.writeFile(filePath, content, 'utf8');
    console.log(`Manuscript ${fileName} saved successfully.`);
  } catch (err) {
    console.error(`Error saving manuscript: ${err.message}`);
  }
}
// Function to read a manuscript using promises
async function readManuscript(fileName) {
  const filePath = path.join(__dirname, 'manuscripts',
fileName);
  try {
    const data = await fs.readFile(filePath, 'utf8');
```

```
    console.log(`Manuscript ${fileName} read successfully.`);
    return data;
  } catch (err) {
    console.error(`Error reading manuscript: ${err.message}`);
    throw err;
  }
}
module.exports = {
  saveManuscript,
  readManuscript,
};
```

- Using Async/Await in Routes

```
// file: routes/manuscriptRoutes.js
// Route to upload a manuscript
router.post('/manuscripts', async (req, res) => {
  const { fileName, content } = req.body;
  await saveManuscript(fileName, content);
  res.status(201).json({ message: 'Manuscript uploaded
successfully.' });
});
// Route to get a manuscript
router.get('/manuscripts/:fileName', async (req, res) => {
  const fileName = req.params.fileName;
  try {
    const data = await readManuscript(fileName);
    res.send(data);
  } catch (err) {
    res.status(500).json({ error: 'Failed to read manuscript.'
});
```

```
  }
});
```

Implementing File Watching

File watching is the solution for monitoring changes in files or directories and responding accordingly. There's no better way to do this than with Node.js's **fs.watch()** and **fs.watchFile()**.

Suppose we have a directory where authors can drop their manuscripts, and we want to process new files automatically, then we should carry out the following steps:

- Setting Up File Watching

```
// file: services/fileWatcher.js
const fs = require('fs');
const path = require('path');
const manuscriptsDir = path.join(__dirname, 'manuscripts');
function startWatching() {
  fs.watch(manuscriptsDir, (eventType, filename) => {
    if (filename) {
      console.log(`Event type: ${eventType}`);
      console.log(`Filename: ${filename}`);
      if (eventType === 'rename') {
        const filePath = path.join(manuscriptsDir, filename);
        fs.stat(filePath, (err, stats) => {
          if (err) {
            // File might have been removed
            console.log(`File ${filename} was removed.`);
          } else {
            if (stats.isFile()) {
              console.log(`New file ${filename} detected.
Processing...`);
              // Process the new file (e.g., parse, validate)
            }
```

```
            }
          });
        }
      } else {
        console.log('Filename not provided');
      }
    });
    console.log(`Watching for changes in ${manuscriptsDir}`);
}
module.exports = {
    startWatching,
};
```

- Starting File Watcher in your application entry point:

```
// file: app.js
const { startWatching } = require('./services/fileWatcher');
// Start watching the manuscripts directory
startWatching();
// ... rest of the server setup
```

The **fs.watch()** function monitors the specified directory for any changes. When a file is added or removed, a rename event is triggered. To determine if the file was added or deleted, **fs.stat()** is used.

- Handling File Changes with Debouncing

File events can sometimes fire multiple times. So let us implement debouncing to handle this.

```
// Modify fileWatcher.js
let debounceTimer = {};
function startWatching() {
    fs.watch(manuscriptsDir, (eventType, filename) => {
      if (filename) {
```

```
      if (debounceTimer[filename]) {
        clearTimeout(debounceTimer[filename]);
      }
      debounceTimer[filename] = setTimeout(() => {
        handleFileEvent(eventType, filename);
        delete debounceTimer[filename];
      }, 100); // Adjust delay as needed
    }
  });
  console.log(`Watching for changes in ${manuscriptsDir}`);
}
function handleFileEvent(eventType, filename) {
  // ... existing logic
}
```

Managing File Permissions

The Node.js file system allows you to control who can read, write, or execute a file using methods like **fs.chmod()** and **fs.chown()**. Suppose we want to ensure that manuscript files are only readable and writable by the owner.

Setting Permissions with 'fs.chmod()'

- Modify the **saveManuscript** function:

```
// file: controllers/fileController.js
async function saveManuscript(fileName, content) {
  const filePath = path.join(__dirname, 'manuscripts',
fileName);
  try {
    await fs.writeFile(filePath, content, 'utf8');
    console.log(`Manuscript ${fileName} saved successfully.`);
    // Set file permissions to read and write for owner only
(0600)
```

```
    await fs.chmod(filePath, 0o600);
    console.log(`Permissions for ${fileName} set to 0600.`);
  } catch (err) {
    console.error(`Error saving manuscript: ${err.message}`);
  }
}
```

After writing the file, we set its permissions using **fs.chmod()**. The mode **0o600** sets the file to be readable and writable by the owner only.

Changing File Ownership with 'fs.chown()'

This method requires appropriate system permissions and is not commonly used in applications running as unprivileged users. However, for completeness:

```
// Change ownership to a specific user and group
await fs.chown(filePath, uid, gid);
```

Replace uid and gid with the user ID and group ID.

Checking File Permissions

We can check the file's permissions using **fs.stat()**.

```
// file: services/fileUtils.js
async function checkPermissions(fileName) {
  const filePath = path.join(__dirname, 'manuscripts',
fileName);
  try {
    const stats = await fs.stat(filePath);
    const mode = stats.mode & 0o777;
    console.log(`Permissions for ${fileName}:
${mode.toString(8)}`);
  } catch (err) {
    console.error(`Error checking permissions:
${err.message}`);
  }
```

```
}
module.exports = {
  checkPermissions,
};
```

Handling Directory Operations

Creating, reading, and deleting directories can be done using methods like **fs.mkdir()**, **fs.readdir()**, and **fs.rmdir()**.

Suppose we want to store manuscripts in directories named after the author.

- Creating Directories Asynchronously

```
// file: controllers/fileController.js
async function saveManuscriptByAuthor(authorName, fileName,
content) {
  const dirPath = path.join(__dirname, 'manuscripts',
authorName);
  const filePath = path.join(dirPath, fileName);
  try {
    // Check if directory exists
    await fs.mkdir(dirPath, { recursive: true });
    // Save the manuscript
    await fs.writeFile(filePath, content, 'utf8');
    console.log(`Manuscript ${fileName} saved under
${authorName}.`);
  } catch (err) {
    console.error(`Error saving manuscript: ${err.message}`);
  }
}
```

fs.mkdir() creates the directory if it does not already exist, with the **recursive: true** option selected. The author's directory is where manuscripts are saved.

- Reading Files in a Directory

```
// file: controllers/fileController.js
async function listManuscriptsByAuthor(authorName) {
  const dirPath = path.join(__dirname, 'manuscripts',
authorName);
  try {
    const files = await fs.readdir(dirPath);
    console.log(`Manuscripts by ${authorName}:`, files);
    return files;
  } catch (err) {
    console.error(`Error listing manuscripts:
${err.message}`);
    throw err;
  }
}
```

- Deleting Files and Directories

```
// Deleting a file
await fs.unlink(filePath);
// Deleting an empty directory
await fs.rmdir(dirPath);
// Deleting a directory recursively (Node.js 12.10+)
await fs.rmdir(dirPath, { recursive: true });
```

Using Streams for Large Files

When dealing with large files, using streams is more efficient than reading or writing the entire file at once. To do this, follow the below:

- Streaming a File to the Client

```
// file: routes/manuscriptRoutes.js
router.get('/manuscripts/:fileName/stream', (req, res) => {
  const fileName = req.params.fileName;
```

```
  const filePath = path.join(__dirname, '../manuscripts',
fileName);
  const readStream = fs.createReadStream(filePath, 'utf8');
  readStream.on('error', (err) => {
    console.error(`Error reading file: ${err.message}`);
    res.status(500).json({ error: 'Failed to read manuscript.'
});
  });
  res.writeHead(200, { 'Content-Type': 'text/plain' });
  readStream.pipe(res);
});
```

We use **fs.createReadStream()** to create a read stream, then pipe it directly to the response. This approach ensures optimal memory efficiency for large files.

- Writing to a File Using a Write Stream

```
// file: controllers/fileController.js
function saveManuscriptStream(fileName, contentStream) {
  const filePath = path.join(__dirname, 'manuscripts',
fileName);
  const writeStream = fs.createWriteStream(filePath, {
encoding: 'utf8' });
  contentStream.pipe(writeStream);
  writeStream.on('finish', () => {
    console.log(`Manuscript ${fileName} saved successfully.`);
  });
  writeStream.on('error', (err) => {
    console.error(`Error writing file: ${err.message}`);
  });
}
```

Our book publishing platform now handles files more efficiently and securely than ever thanks to our expertise in advanced Node.js file system operations. We know how to perform asynchronous file operations, implement file watching to monitor changes and manage file permissions to protect sensitive data.

Mastering Streams for Efficient Data Processing

In this section, we'll explore how to use Node.js streams—specifically readable, writable, duplex, and transform streams—to process data efficiently in our book publishing platform. Streams allow us to handle data piece by piece, without keeping it all in memory, which is especially useful when dealing with large files or data streams.

Understanding Streams

Streams are objects that allow reading data from a source or writing data to a destination in a continuous fashion. There are four types of streams in Node.js:

- **Readable Streams**: Stream data for reading.
- **Writable Streams**: Stream data for writing.
- **Duplex Streams**: Streams that are both readable and writable.
- **Transform Streams**: Duplex streams that can modify or transform the data as it is read or written.

Using Readable Streams

We'll start by reading large manuscript files using readable streams. We need to serve large manuscript files to clients without loading the entire file into memory.

- Implementing a Readable Stream

```
// file: routes/manuscriptRoutes.js
const express = require('express');
const router = express.Router();
const fs = require('fs');
const path = require('path');
// Route to stream a manuscript
router.get('/manuscripts/:fileName/stream', (req, res) => {
  const fileName = req.params.fileName;
  const filePath = path.join(__dirname, '../manuscripts',
fileName);
```

```
  // Check if the file exists
  fs.access(filePath, fs.constants.F_OK, (err) => {
    if (err) {
      console.error(`File not found: ${fileName}`);
      return res.status(404).json({ error: 'Manuscript not
found.' });
    }
    // Create a readable stream
    const readStream = fs.createReadStream(filePath, {
encoding: 'utf8' });
    // Handle errors
    readStream.on('error', (err) => {
      console.error(`Error reading file: ${err.message}`);
      res.status(500).json({ error: 'Failed to read
manuscript.' });
    });
    // Set appropriate headers
    res.setHeader('Content-Type', 'text/plain');
    // Pipe the stream to the response
    readStream.pipe(res);
  });
});
module.exports = router;
```

We create a readable stream using **fs.createReadStream()**. This method produces the most reliable, readable stream. We pipe the stream directly to the HTTP response using **readStream.pipe(res)**. This method is the most efficient and non-blocking way to handle large files.

Using Writable Streams

Writable streams allow us to write data efficiently. Suppose we want to save uploaded manuscript files sent from the client.

- Implementing a Writable Stream

First, we'll use middleware to handle file uploads. We'll use the **multer** package for handling multipart/form-data.

```
npm install multer
```

- Setting Up Multer for File Uploads

```
// file: middleware/upload.js
const multer = require('multer');
const path = require('path');
const storage = multer.diskStorage({
  destination: function (req, file, cb) {
    cb(null, path.join(__dirname, '../manuscripts'));
  },
  filename: function (req, file, cb) {
    cb(null, file.originalname);
  },
});
const upload = multer({ storage: storage });
module.exports = upload;
```

- Updating the Route to Handle File Uploads

```
// file: routes/manuscriptRoutes.js
const upload = require('../middleware/upload');
// Route to upload a manuscript
router.post('/manuscripts/upload',
upload.single('manuscript'), (req, res) => {
  res.status(201).json({ message: 'Manuscript uploaded
successfully.' });
});
```

The **multer** middleware handles the file upload and saves it to the specified directory. Under the hood, **multer** uses writable streams to write the uploaded file to disk.

- Writing a File Manually Using a Writable Stream

If we wanted to write the file manually, we could read the uploaded file as a stream and write it using a writable stream.

```
// file: routes/manuscriptRoutes.js
router.post('/manuscripts/upload', (req, res) => {
  const fileName = req.headers['file-name'];
  const filePath = path.join(__dirname, '../manuscripts',
fileName);
  // Create a writable stream
  const writeStream = fs.createWriteStream(filePath);
  // Pipe the request data to the write stream
  req.pipe(writeStream);
  req.on('end', () => {
    res.status(201).json({ message: 'Manuscript uploaded
successfully.' });
  });
  req.on('error', (err) => {
    console.error(`Error uploading file: ${err.message}`);
    res.status(500).json({ error: 'Failed to upload
manuscript.' });
  });
});
```

This method assumes that the client is sending the file data directly in the request body, which may not be practical.

Using Duplex Streams

Duplex streams are both readable and writable. They are useful when you need to read and write data simultaneously.

Suppose we have a requirement to proxy data between two network streams.

- Implementing a Simple Duplex Stream

```
// file: services/proxyStream.js
```

```
const { Duplex } = require('stream');
class ProxyStream extends Duplex {
  constructor(options) {
    super(options);
  }
  _read(size) {
    // Implement reading data
  }
  _write(chunk, encoding, callback) {
    // Implement writing data
    this.push(chunk); // Echo data back
    callback();
  }
}
module.exports = ProxyStream;
```

We create a custom duplex stream by extending the **Duplex** class. We implement the **_read** and **_write** methods. In this example, the stream echoes back any data written to it.

Using Transform Streams

The transform stream is a duplex stream that modifies the data as it passes through. For example, suppose we want to encrypt manuscript files before we save them.

Using Crypto Module with Transform Streams

We'll use the **crypto** module to create a cipher, which is a type of transform stream.

```
// file: controllers/fileController.js
const crypto = require('crypto');
function encryptStream(password) {
  return crypto.createCipher('aes-256-cbc', password);
}
function decryptStream(password) {
```

```
  return crypto.createDecipher('aes-256-cbc', password);
}
```

Now, updating the save manuscript function

```
// file: controllers/fileController.js
function saveEncryptedManuscript(fileName, content, password)
{
  const filePath = path.join(__dirname, 'manuscripts',
fileName);
  const writeStream = fs.createWriteStream(filePath);
  const cipher = encryptStream(password);
  // Convert content to a readable stream
  const { Readable } = require('stream');
  const readStream = new Readable();
  readStream.push(content);
  readStream.push(null); // Signal end of stream
  // Pipe the streams: read -> cipher -> write
  readStream.pipe(cipher).pipe(writeStream);
  writeStream.on('finish', () => {
    console.log(`Encrypted manuscript ${fileName} saved
successfully.`);
  });
  writeStream.on('error', (err) => {
    console.error(`Error writing file: ${err.message}`);
  });
}
```

We create a readable stream from the content using **crypto.createCipher()**. We then pipe the readable stream through the cipher and then to the writable stream. This encrypts the data before writing it to disk.

Reading and Decrypting Manuscript

```
// file: controllers/fileController.js
function readEncryptedManuscript(fileName, password, res) {
  const filePath = path.join(__dirname, 'manuscripts',
fileName);
  const readStream = fs.createReadStream(filePath);
  const decipher = decryptStream(password);
  // Pipe the streams: read -> decipher -> response
  readStream.pipe(decipher).pipe(res);
  readStream.on('error', (err) => {
    console.error(`Error reading file: ${err.message}`);
    res.status(500).json({ error: 'Failed to read manuscript.'
});
  });
}
```

Next, updating the route to read encrypted manuscripts.

```
// file: routes/manuscriptRoutes.js
router.get('/manuscripts/:fileName/encrypted', (req, res) => {
  const fileName = req.params.fileName;
  const password = req.query.password;
  if (!password) {
    return res.status(400).json({ error: 'Password is
required.' });
  }
  readEncryptedManuscript(fileName, password, res);
});
```

Handling Backpressure

When you're working with streams, it's important to handle backpressure. This is when the destination you can write to can't keep up with the source you can read from.

For example, you can pause and resume streams in a number of different ways.

```
readStream.on('data', (chunk) => {
  const canWrite = writeStream.write(chunk);
  if (!canWrite) {
    // Pause the read stream if the write buffer is full
    readStream.pause();
  }
});
writeStream.on('drain', () => {
  // Resume the read stream when the write buffer is drained
  readStream.resume();
});
```

In the example above, we're listening for the drain event on the writable stream, which means it can accept more data. We pause the readable stream when the writable stream's buffer is full and resume it when it's ready.

Piping Multiple Streams

We can combine multiple streams using the **pipe()** method. For example, we can compress and encrypt a manuscript.

```
// file: controllers/fileController.js
const zlib = require('zlib');
function saveCompressedEncryptedManuscript(fileName, content,
password) {
  const filePath = path.join(__dirname, 'manuscripts',
fileName);
  const writeStream = fs.createWriteStream(filePath);
  const gzip = zlib.createGzip();
  const cipher = encryptStream(password);
  const { Readable } = require('stream');
  const readStream = new Readable();
  readStream.push(content);
```

```
  readStream.push(null);
  // Pipe the streams: read -> gzip -> cipher -> write
  readStream.pipe(gzip).pipe(cipher).pipe(writeStream);
  writeStream.on('finish', () => {
    console.log(`Compressed and encrypted manuscript
${fileName} saved successfully.`);
  });
  writeStream.on('error', (err) => {
    console.error(`Error writing file: ${err.message}`);
  });
}
```

Here, we use **zlib.createGzip()** to compress the data. Next, we join all the data streams together so they'll compress, encrypt then write the data in that order.

By getting to grips with streams, we've been able to process data super efficiently on our book publishing platform. We've implemented streams that are readable, writable, duplex, and transformable, which help us to handle large files, encrypt data, and transform content on the fly.

Creating Custom Stream Implementations

Understanding Custom Streams

Custom streams allow us to encapsulate complex data transformations and processing logic in a modular and reusable way. By building our own stream implementations, we can tailor the data flow to suit the unique needs of our application.

As previously discussed, Node.js provides four types of streams:

- **Readable Streams**: Streams from which data can be read.
- **Writable Streams**: Streams to which data can be written.
- **Duplex Streams**: Streams that are both readable and writable.
- **Transform Streams**: Duplex streams that can modify or transform the data as it is read or written.

By building on these base classes from the Stream module, we can create our own custom streams that have specific behaviors.

Creating a Custom Transform Stream

Suppose our book publishing platform needs to perform text analysis on manuscripts, such as counting word frequency, detecting prohibited content, or formatting text according to specific guidelines. We can create custom transform streams to process the manuscript data as it flows through the system. So, let's create a custom transform stream that counts the frequency of each word in a manuscript.

```
// file: transforms/wordFrequencyTransform.js
const { Transform } = require('stream');
class WordFrequencyTransform extends Transform {
  constructor(options) {
    super(options);
    this.wordCounts = {};
    this.remainingChunk = '';
  }
  _transform(chunk, encoding, callback) {
    let data = this.remainingChunk + chunk.toString();
    const words = data.split(/\s+/);
    // Save the last word in case it's incomplete
    this.remainingChunk = words.pop();
    words.forEach((word) => {
      const cleanedWord = word.toLowerCase().replace(/[^\w]/g,
'');
      if (cleanedWord) {
        this.wordCounts[cleanedWord] =
(this.wordCounts[cleanedWord] || 0) + 1;
      }
    });
    callback();
  }
  _flush(callback) {
    // Process any remaining data
    if (this.remainingChunk) {
```

```
      const cleanedWord =
this.remainingChunk.toLowerCase().replace(/[^\w]/g, '');
      if (cleanedWord) {
        this.wordCounts[cleanedWord] =
(this.wordCounts[cleanedWord] || 0) + 1;
      }
    }
    // Emit the word counts as a JSON string
    this.push(JSON.stringify(this.wordCounts));
    callback();
  }
}
module.exports = WordFrequencyTransform;
```

Here's how it works:

- The **constructor** initializes the wordCounts object to keep track of word frequencies and a remainingChunk string to handle incomplete words at the chunk boundaries.
- Then, the **_transform** processes each chunk of data. It concatenates any leftover data from the previous chunk, splits the data into words, and updates the word counts.
- Finally, the **_flush** is called when there's no more data to be consumed. It processes any remaining data and pushes the final result downstream.

Now, we can use this transform stream to analyze a manuscript as it's being read.

```
// file: controllers/analysisController.js
const fs = require('fs');
const path = require('path');
const WordFrequencyTransform =
require('../transforms/wordFrequencyTransform');
async function analyzeManuscript(fileName) {
  const filePath = path.join(__dirname, '../manuscripts',
fileName);
  return new Promise((resolve, reject) => {
```

```
    const readStream = fs.createReadStream(filePath, {
encoding: 'utf8' });
    const wordFrequency = new WordFrequencyTransform();
    let result = '';
    wordFrequency.on('data', (data) => {
      result += data;
    });
    wordFrequency.on('end', () => {
      const wordCounts = JSON.parse(result);
      resolve(wordCounts);
    });
    wordFrequency.on('error', (err) => {
      reject(err);
    });
    readStream.pipe(wordFrequency);
  });
}
module.exports = {
  analyzeManuscript,
};
```

Creating Route to Perform Analysis

```
// file: routes/analysisRoutes.js
const express = require('express');
const router = express.Router();
const { analyzeManuscript } =
require('../controllers/analysisController');
router.get('/manuscripts/:fileName/analysis', async (req, res)
=> {
  const fileName = req.params.fileName;
```

```
  try {
    const wordCounts = await analyzeManuscript(fileName);
    res.json(wordCounts);
  } catch (err) {
    console.error(`Error analyzing manuscript:
${err.message}`);
    res.status(500).json({ error: 'Failed to analyze
manuscript.' });
  }
});
module.exports = router;
```

Here,

- We define an endpoint **/manuscripts/:fileName/analysis** to perform the word frequency analysis.
- The **analyzeManuscript** function reads the file, pipes it through the **WordFrequencyTransform**, and returns the word counts.

Creating a Custom Writable Stream

Suppose we need to write logs to a database instead of the file system.

```
// file: streams/databaseWritable.js
const { Writable } = require('stream');
const db = require('../database'); // Hypothetical database
module
class DatabaseWritable extends Writable {
  constructor(options) {
    super(options);
  }
  _write(chunk, encoding, callback) {
    const logEntry = chunk.toString();
    // Simulate writing to a database
    db.insertLog(logEntry)
```

```
      .then(() => callback())
      .catch((err) => callback(err));
  }
}
module.exports = DatabaseWritable;
```

This is where we use the **_write** function to save the data to the stream. We then convert the chunk to a string and add it to the database.

Creating a Custom Duplex Stream

Suppose we need a stream that can both read data from a source and write transformed data to a destination, perhaps for a network proxy or data processor.

So here, we'll create a duplex stream that reads data line by line and writes each line reversed.

```
// file: streams/lineReverser.js
const { Duplex } = require('stream');
class LineReverser extends Duplex {
  constructor(options) {
    super(options);
    this.buffer = '';
  }
  _write(chunk, encoding, callback) {
    this.buffer += chunk.toString();
    const lines = this.buffer.split('\n');
    this.buffer = lines.pop(); // Keep the last partial line
    lines.forEach((line) => {
      const reversedLine = line.split('').reverse().join('');
      this.push(reversedLine + '\n');
    });
    callback();
  }
```

```
  _read(size) {
    // No implementation needed if data is pushed synchronously in _write
  }
  _final(callback) {
    // Process any remaining data
    if (this.buffer) {
      const reversedLine = this.buffer.split('').reverse().join('');
      this.push(reversedLine + '\n');
    }
    this.push(null);
    callback();
  }
}
module.exports = LineReverser;
```

Here's what happens in the above code:

- **_write** handles incoming data, processes complete lines, reverses them, and sends them to read.
- **_read** is unnecessary because we send data in real time.
- **_final** processes any remaining data when the writeable side ends.

Next, we use the **LineReverser** stream as below:

```
// file: controllers/fileController.js
const LineReverser = require('../streams/lineReverser');
function reverseLinesInManuscript(fileName) {
  const filePath = path.join(__dirname, '../manuscripts', fileName);
  const outputFilePath = path.join(__dirname, '../manuscripts', `reversed_${fileName}`);
  const readStream = fs.createReadStream(filePath, { encoding: 'utf8' });
```

```
  const writeStream = fs.createWriteStream(outputFilePath);
  const lineReverser = new LineReverser();
  readStream.pipe(lineReverser).pipe(writeStream);
  return new Promise((resolve, reject) => {
    writeStream.on('finish', () => {
      console.log(`Reversed lines saved to
${outputFilePath}`);
      resolve();
    });
    writeStream.on('error', (err) => {
      console.error(`Error writing file: ${err.message}`);
      reject(err);
    });
  });
}
module.exports = {
  reverseLinesInManuscript,
};
```

we finally create a route to trigger the line reversable:

```
// file: routes/manuscriptRoutes.js
const { reverseLinesInManuscript } =
require('../controllers/fileController');
router.post('/manuscripts/:fileName/reverse-lines', async
(req, res) => {
  const fileName = req.params.fileName;
  try {
    await reverseLinesInManuscript(fileName);
    res.status(200).json({ message: 'Lines reversed
successfully.' });
  } catch (err) {
```

```
    res.status(500).json({ error: 'Failed to reverse lines in manuscript.' });
  }
});
module.exports = router;
```

Custom Readable Stream

Suppose we need to generate data on the fly, such as creating a report or streaming synthetic data. For this, first implement the **RandomTextStream** class:

```
// file: streams/randomTextStream.js
const { Readable } = require('stream');
class RandomTextStream extends Readable {
  constructor(options) {
    super(options);
    this.sentences = [
      'The quick brown fox jumps over the lazy dog.',
      'Lorem ipsum dolor sit amet, consectetur adipiscing elit.',
      'Node.js streams are powerful.',
      'Custom streams allow for flexible data processing.',
    ];
    this.index = 0;
  }
  _read(size) {
    if (this.index >= this.sentences.length) {
      this.push(null); // No more data
    } else {
      const sentence = this.sentences[this.index];
      this.push(sentence + '\n');
      this.index += 1;
```

```
    }
  }
}
module.exports = RandomTextStream;
```

Next, putting the **RandomTextStream** into use:

```
// file: routes/dataRoutes.js
const RandomTextStream =
require('../streams/randomTextStream');
const express = require('express');
const router = express.Router();
router.get('/random-text', (req, res) => {
  const randomTextStream = new RandomTextStream();
  res.setHeader('Content-Type', 'text/plain');
  randomTextStream.pipe(res);
  randomTextStream.on('error', (err) => {
    console.error(`Error in random text stream:
${err.message}`);
    res.status(500).end('Internal Server Error');
  });
});
module.exports = router;
```

Here, we create a route **/random-text** that streams random sentences to the client. The **RandomTextStream** generates data dynamically without reading from any source.

By building our own stream implementations, we've made it possible to process data in more advanced ways that are specific to what we need. It doesn't matter if we're analyzing text, transforming content, or integrating with other systems—custom streams are a great way to make data processing more efficient and flexible in Node.js applications.

Managing Large Data Sets with Buffers

Buffers are really important when we're working with binary data, like files, network packets, or any kind of raw data streams. When we use buffers, we can make better use of our memory and improve how quickly our book publishing platform works, especially when we're processing lots of data, like large manuscripts or lots of multimedia content.

Understanding Buffers in Node.js

A Buffer is a fixed-size chunk of memory allocated outside of the V8 JavaScript engine. It allows Node.js to handle binary data efficiently. Buffers are instances of the **Buffer** class, which is a global object in Node.js, making it available without importing any modules.

Why Use Buffers?

- JavaScript strings are designed for Unicode text, not binary data. Buffers enable us to work with raw binary data.
- Buffers allow us to process data in chunks, reducing memory overhead and avoiding blocking the event loop.
- Streams often emit data as Buffers, so understanding how to manipulate them is crucial.

Suppose our book publishing platform needs to handle large image files for book covers or process large binary files like PDFs. We'll demonstrate how to use Buffers to optimize memory usage and performance.

Reading Large Files using Buffers

When reading large files, we should avoid loading the entire file into memory. Instead, we'll read the file in chunks using Buffers.

```
// file: controllers/imageController.js
const fs = require('fs');
const path = require('path');
function readLargeImage(fileName, res) {
  const filePath = path.join(__dirname, 'images', fileName);
  // Create a readable stream
  const readStream = fs.createReadStream(filePath);
  // Handle errors
  readStream.on('error', (err) => {
    console.error(`Error reading image: ${err.message}`);
    res.status(500).json({ error: 'Failed to read image.' });
  });
```

```
  // Set appropriate headers
  res.setHeader('Content-Type', 'image/jpeg');
  // Pipe the stream to the response
  readStream.pipe(res);
}
module.exports = {
  readLargeImage,
};
```

In the above, we use **fs.createReadStream()** to read the file in chunks. Each chunk is a Buffer containing a portion of the file's binary data. We then pipe the read stream directly to the HTTP response, which efficiently streams the image to the client without loading it entirely into memory.

Writing Large Files using Buffers

When we're working with large files, we can save data in chunks using buffers to avoid using too much memory. For instance, let's say we're saving a large uploaded file.

```
// file: routes/imageRoutes.js
const express = require('express');
const router = express.Router();
const fs = require('fs');
const path = require('path');
// Middleware to handle file uploads
const multer = require('multer');
const storage = multer.memoryStorage(); // Store file in memory temporarily
const upload = multer({ storage: storage });
router.post('/images/upload', upload.single('image'), (req, res) => {
  const fileBuffer = req.file.buffer; // Buffer containing the file data
  const fileName = req.file.originalname;
```

```
  const filePath = path.join(__dirname, '../images',
fileName);
  // Create a writable stream
  const writeStream = fs.createWriteStream(filePath);
  // Write the buffer to the file
  writeStream.write(fileBuffer, () => {
    console.log(`Image ${fileName} saved successfully.`);
    res.status(201).json({ message: 'Image uploaded
successfully.' });
  });
  writeStream.on('error', (err) => {
    console.error(`Error writing image: ${err.message}`);
    res.status(500).json({ error: 'Failed to save image.' });
  });
});
module.exports = router;
```

Here in the above program, we use **multer** with **memoryStorage** to handle the file upload, which provides the file data as a Buffer. We create a writable stream to write the file to disk.

Now here, writing the Buffer directly to the file is efficient for small to medium-sized files. So for very large files, it's better to stream the data directly to the file system to avoid keeping the entire file in memory.

So, if you're working with large files, it's better to stream the data instead of buffering the whole file.

```
router.post('/images/upload', (req, res) => {
  const fileName = req.headers['file-name'];
  const filePath = path.join(__dirname, '../images',
fileName);
  // Create a writable stream
  const writeStream = fs.createWriteStream(filePath);
  // Pipe the request stream directly to the file
  req.pipe(writeStream);
```

```
  writeStream.on('finish', () => {
    console.log(`Image ${fileName} saved successfully.`);
    res.status(201).json({ message: 'Image uploaded
successfully.' });
  });
  writeStream.on('error', (err) => {
    console.error(`Error writing image: ${err.message}`);
    res.status(500).json({ error: 'Failed to save image.' });
  });
});
```

This approach avoids loading the entire file into memory, making it suitable for large files.

Manipulating Binary Data with Buffers

Suppose we need to process binary data, such as resizing an image or manipulating PDF files. So here, we'll use the **sharp** library, which uses Buffers to process images efficiently.

We've already got the Sharp library up and running on the system, and there's a pretty good explanation of how to do that in one of the previous chapters. So let's move on to processing an image buffer.

```
// file: controllers/imageController.js
const sharp = require('sharp');
async function resizeImage(fileBuffer, width, height) {
  try {
    const resizedBuffer = await sharp(fileBuffer)
      .resize(width, height)
      .toBuffer();
    return resizedBuffer;
  } catch (err) {
    console.error(`Error resizing image: ${err.message}`);
    throw err;
  }
```

```
}
```

Here, we pass the image Buffer to **sharp**, which processes the image in memory using Buffers. The result is a new Buffer containing the resized image.

Next, we use the function in a route:

```
// file: routes/imageRoutes.js
router.post('/images/upload-resize', upload.single('image'),
async (req, res) => {
  const fileBuffer = req.file.buffer;
  const fileName = `resized_${req.file.originalname}`;
  const filePath = path.join(__dirname, '../images',
fileName);
  try {
    const resizedBuffer = await resizeImage(fileBuffer, 800,
600);
    // Write the resized image to disk
    fs.writeFile(filePath, resizedBuffer, (err) => {
      if (err) {
        console.error(`Error saving resized image:
${err.message}`);
        return res.status(500).json({ error: 'Failed to save
resized image.' });
      }
      console.log(`Resized image ${fileName} saved
successfully.`);
      res.status(201).json({ message: 'Image uploaded and
resized successfully.' });
    });
  } catch (err) {
    res.status(500).json({ error: 'Failed to resize image.'
});
  }
```

```
});
```

Instead of reading the entire file into memory, we can process the image in streams.

```
// file: controllers/imageController.js
function resizeImageStream(readStream, width, height) {
  return readStream.pipe(sharp().resize(width, height));
}
```

Using the function in a route:

```
// file: routes/imageRoutes.js
router.post('/images/upload-resize', (req, res) => {
  const fileName = req.headers['file-name'];
  const filePath = path.join(__dirname, '../images',
`resized_${fileName}`);
  const writeStream = fs.createWriteStream(filePath);
  const resizeStream = resizeImageStream(req, 800, 600);
  resizeStream.pipe(writeStream);
  writeStream.on('finish', () => {
    console.log(`Resized image ${fileName} saved
successfully.`);
    res.status(201).json({ message: 'Image uploaded and
resized successfully.' });
  });
  writeStream.on('error', (err) => {
    console.error(`Error saving resized image:
${err.message}`);
    res.status(500).json({ error: 'Failed to save resized
image.' });
  });
});
```

Here's how we can benefit:

- By chunking the data and not loading the whole file into memory, we'll get better memory efficiency.
- Stream processing can be faster with less resource-intensive processing.

Concatenating Buffers

When working with data received in chunks, we may need to concatenate Buffers. Let's look at an example of gathering data from a stream.

```
// Collect data from a readable stream
function collectStreamData(stream, callback) {
  const chunks = [];
  stream.on('data', (chunk) => {
    chunks.push(chunk);
  });
  stream.on('end', () => {
    const data = Buffer.concat(chunks);
    callback(null, data);
  });
  stream.on('error', (err) => {
    callback(err);
  });
}
```

Here,

- We collect chunks of data emitted from the stream.
- We use **`Buffer.concat()`** to combine the chunks into a single Buffer.
- This is useful when we need the complete data, such as parsing a JSON payload received in chunks.

Working with Binary Protocols

Suppose we need to handle binary data from network protocols or perform low-level data manipulation.

Let's assume we have a binary file format where:

- The first 4 bytes represent an integer (file version).

- The next 8 bytes represent a double (timestamp).
- The remaining bytes are a UTF-8 encoded string (content).

Let us perform parsing on the binary file:

```
// file: controllers/binaryFileController.js
function parseBinaryFile(filePath, callback) {
  fs.readFile(filePath, (err, data) => {
    if (err) return callback(err);
    let offset = 0;
    // Read 4-byte integer
    const version = data.readInt32BE(offset);
    offset += 4;
    // Read 8-byte double
    const timestamp = data.readDoubleBE(offset);
    offset += 8;
    // Read the remaining bytes as a string
    const content = data.toString('utf8', offset);
    callback(null, { version, timestamp, content });
  });
}
module.exports = {
  parseBinaryFile,
};
```

In the above code,

- We use methods like **`readInt32BE`** and **`readDoubleBE`** to read integers and doubles from the Buffer.
- We specify the byte offset to keep track of our position in the Buffer.
- This approach allows precise control over binary data parsing.

These techniques help us keep our application responsive and scalable, even when we're dealing with a lot of data. It's important to keep an eye on memory usage, handle errors in a way that doesn't slow things down, and manage data flow to prevent bottlenecks and memory leaks.

Integrating Crypto Module for Data Security

Introduction to Crypto Module

The **crypto** module provides cryptographic functionalities, including hashing, encryption/decryption using cipher algorithms, and secure random number generation. The **crypto** module is a built-in Node.js module that offers a comprehensive suite of cryptographic functions. It allows developers to implement secure data handling practices without relying on external libraries.

The key functionalities include:

- Creating fixed-size representations of data, useful for password storage and data integrity checks.
- Encrypting and decrypting data to protect sensitive information during storage or transmission.
- Generating cryptographically strong random values for tokens, keys, and other security-related purposes.

Hashing with Crypto Module

Hashing is a one-way process that converts data into a fixed-size string of characters, which is typically used to store passwords securely. Instead of storing plain-text passwords, we store their hashed equivalents, enhancing security by preventing unauthorized access even if the database is compromised.

We'll create a user registration system where passwords are hashed before being stored.

```
// file: models/userModel.js
const users = [];
function addUser(username, hashedPassword) {
  users.push({ username, hashedPassword });
}
function findUser(username) {
  return users.find(user => user.username === username);
}
module.exports = {
  addUser,
  findUser,
```

```
};
```

We'll use the **crypto** module's **pbkdf2** function to hash passwords securely.

```
// file: controllers/authController.js
const crypto = require('crypto');
const { addUser, findUser } = require('../models/userModel');
// Function to hash a password
function hashPassword(password) {
  return new Promise((resolve, reject) => {
    const salt = crypto.randomBytes(16).toString('hex');
    const iterations = 100000;
    const keylen = 64;
    const digest = 'sha512';
    crypto.pbkdf2(password, salt, iterations, keylen, digest,
(err, derivedKey) => {
      if (err) reject(err);
      resolve(`${salt}:${derivedKey.toString('hex')}`);
    });
  });
}
// Function to verify a password
function verifyPassword(password, hashedPassword) {
  return new Promise((resolve, reject) => {
    const [salt, key] = hashedPassword.split(':');
    const iterations = 100000;
    const keylen = 64;
    const digest = 'sha512';
    crypto.pbkdf2(password, salt, iterations, keylen, digest,
(err, derivedKey) => {
      if (err) reject(err);
```

```
      resolve(key === derivedKey.toString('hex'));
    });
  });
}
// Registration handler
async function register(req, res) {
  const { username, password } = req.body;
  if (findUser(username)) {
    return res.status(400).json({ error: 'User already
exists.' });
  }
  try {
    const hashedPassword = await hashPassword(password);
    addUser(username, hashedPassword);
    res.status(201).json({ message: 'User registered
successfully.' });
  } catch (err) {
    res.status(500).json({ error: 'Error registering user.'
});
  }
}
// Login handler
async function login(req, res) {
  const { username, password } = req.body;
  const user = findUser(username);
  if (!user) {
    return res.status(400).json({ error: 'Invalid username or
password.' });
  }
  try {
```

```
    const isValid = await verifyPassword(password,
user.hashedPassword);
    if (isValid) {
      res.status(200).json({ message: 'Login successful.' });
    } else {
      res.status(400).json({ error: 'Invalid username or
password.' });
    }
  } catch (err) {
    res.status(500).json({ error: 'Error logging in.' });
  }
}
module.exports = {
  register,
  login,
};
```

Next, integrating routes into the server

```
// file: app.js
const express = require('express');
const https = require('https');
const fs = require('fs');
const path = require('path');
const WebSocket = require('ws');
const authRoutes = require('./routes/authRoutes');
// ... other imports
const app = express();
// Middleware
app.use(express.json());
// Routes
```

```
app.use('/auth', authRoutes);
// ... other routes
// SSL options
const sslOptions = {
  key: fs.readFileSync(path.join(__dirname, 'server.key')),
  cert: fs.readFileSync(path.join(__dirname, 'server.crt')),
};
// Create HTTPS server
const server = https.createServer(sslOptions, app);
// Create WebSocket server
const wss = new WebSocket.Server({ server });
// ... WebSocket setup
// Start the server
const HTTPS_PORT = process.env.HTTPS_PORT || 3000;
server.listen(HTTPS_PORT, () => {
  console.log(`HTTPS Server is running on port
${HTTPS_PORT}`);
});
```

Next, you can use **curl** or a tool like Postman to test the endpoints.

```
curl -k -X POST -H "Content-Type: application/json" -d
'{"username":"john_doe","password":"securepassword"}'
https://localhost:3000/auth/register
```

Finally, login with the registered user:

```
curl -k -X POST -H "Content-Type: application/json" -d
'{"username":"john_doe","password":"securepassword"}'
https://localhost:3000/auth/login
```

Encrypting and Decrypting Data with Cipher Algorithms

Encryption ensures that sensitive data remains confidential during storage or transmission. We'll implement encryption and decryption of manuscript content using cipher algorithms provided by the **crypto** module.

Setting up Encryption and Decryption Functions

We'll use the AES-256-CBC cipher for symmetric encryption, which requires a secret key and an initialization vector (IV).

```
// file: controllers/cryptoController.js
const crypto = require('crypto');
// Secret key and IV generation
const algorithm = 'aes-256-cbc';
const secretKey = crypto.randomBytes(32); // 256 bits key
const iv = crypto.randomBytes(16); // 128 bits IV
// Function to encrypt data
function encrypt(text) {
  const cipher = crypto.createCipheriv(algorithm, secretKey,
iv);
  let encrypted = cipher.update(text, 'utf8', 'hex');
  encrypted += cipher.final('hex');
  return encrypted;
}
// Function to decrypt data
function decrypt(encryptedText) {
  const decipher = crypto.createDecipheriv(algorithm,
secretKey, iv);
  let decrypted = decipher.update(encryptedText, 'hex',
'utf8');
  decrypted += decipher.final('utf8');
  return decrypted;
}
module.exports = {
  encrypt,
  decrypt,
```

```
  secretKey, // In a real application, store securely
  iv,
};
```

Encrypting and Upload Manuscripts

We'll modify our manuscript saving process to encrypt the content before writing it to disk.

```
// file: controllers/fileController.js
const { encrypt } = require('./cryptoController');
// ... other imports
async function saveEncryptedManuscript(fileName, content) {
  const filePath = path.join(__dirname, 'manuscripts',
fileName);
  try {
    const encryptedContent = encrypt(content);
    await fs.writeFile(filePath, encryptedContent, 'utf8');
    console.log(`Encrypted manuscript ${fileName} saved
successfully.`);
  } catch (err) {
    console.error(`Error saving encrypted manuscript:
${err.message}`);
    throw err;
  }
}
module.exports = {
  saveManuscript,
  readManuscript,
  saveEncryptedManuscript,
};
```

Then creating a route to upload encrypted manuscripts

```
// file: routes/manuscriptRoutes.js
const { saveEncryptedManuscript } =
require('../controllers/fileController');
const express = require('express');
const router = express.Router();
// Route to upload an encrypted manuscript
router.post('/manuscripts/encrypted/upload', async (req, res)
=> {
  const { fileName, content } = req.body;
  try {
    await saveEncryptedManuscript(fileName, content);
    res.status(201).json({ message: 'Encrypted manuscript
uploaded successfully.' });
  } catch (err) {
    res.status(500).json({ error: 'Failed to upload encrypted
manuscript.' });
  }
});
module.exports = router;
```

Decrypting Manuscripts for Retrieval

```
// file: controllers/fileController.js
const { decrypt } = require('./cryptoController');
// ... other imports
async function readEncryptedManuscript(fileName) {
  const filePath = path.join(__dirname, 'manuscripts',
fileName);
  try {
    const encryptedContent = await fs.readFile(filePath,
'utf8');
    const decryptedContent = decrypt(encryptedContent);
```

```
    console.log(`Manuscript ${fileName} decrypted
successfully.`);
    return decryptedContent;
  } catch (err) {
    console.error(`Error reading encrypted manuscript:
${err.message}`);
    throw err;
  }
}
module.exports = {
  saveManuscript,
  readManuscript,
  saveEncryptedManuscript,
  readEncryptedManuscript,
};
// file: routes/manuscriptRoutes.js
const { readEncryptedManuscript } =
require('../controllers/fileController');
const express = require('express');
const router = express.Router();
// Route to get a decrypted manuscript
router.get('/manuscripts/encrypted/:fileName', async (req,
res) => {
  const fileName = req.params.fileName;
  try {
    const decryptedContent = await
readEncryptedManuscript(fileName);
    res.send(decryptedContent);
  } catch (err) {
    res.status(500).json({ error: 'Failed to read encrypted
manuscript.' });
```

```
  }
});
module.exports = router;
```

Testing Encryption and Decryption

First, upload an encrypted manuscript:

```
curl -k -X POST -H "Content-Type: application/json" -d
'{"fileName":"encrypted_book.txt","content":"This is a secret
manuscript."}'
https://localhost:3000/manuscripts/encrypted/upload
```

Following is the expected response:

```
{
  "message": "Encrypted manuscript uploaded successfully."
}
```

Next, retrieve and decrypt the manuscript:

```
curl -k
https://localhost:3000/manuscripts/encrypted/encrypted_book.tx
t
```

You may get the following responses:

```
This is a secret manuscript.
```

Encrypting Sensitive Data in Files

Beyond user passwords, we may need to encrypt other sensitive data, such as user profiles or confidential manuscripts.

So here, we'll create a function to encrypt any file's content before saving it.

```
// file: controllers/fileController.js
const { encrypt, decrypt } = require('./cryptoController');
// ... other imports
async function saveEncryptedData(fileName, data) {
```

```
  const filePath = path.join(__dirname, 'secureData',
fileName);
  try {
    const encryptedData = encrypt(data);
    await fs.writeFile(filePath, encryptedData, 'utf8');
    console.log(`Encrypted data ${fileName} saved
successfully.`);
  } catch (err) {
    console.error(`Error saving encrypted data:
${err.message}`);
    throw err;
  }
}
async function readEncryptedData(fileName) {
  const filePath = path.join(__dirname, 'secureData',
fileName);
  try {
    const encryptedData = await fs.readFile(filePath, 'utf8');
    const decryptedData = decrypt(encryptedData);
    console.log(`Encrypted data ${fileName} decrypted
successfully.`);
    return decryptedData;
  } catch (err) {
    console.error(`Error reading encrypted data:
${err.message}`);
    throw err;
  }
}
module.exports = {
  saveManuscript,
  readManuscript,
```

```
  saveEncryptedManuscript,
  readEncryptedManuscript,
  saveEncryptedData,
  readEncryptedData,
};
```

Next, creating routes for encrypted data as taught earlier.

```
// file: routes/dataRoutes.js
const express = require('express');
const router = express.Router();
const { saveEncryptedData, readEncryptedData } =
require('../controllers/fileController');
// Route to save encrypted data
router.post('/secure-data/save', async (req, res) => {
  const { fileName, data } = req.body;
  try {
    await saveEncryptedData(fileName, data);
    res.status(201).json({ message: 'Encrypted data saved
successfully.' });
  } catch (err) {
    res.status(500).json({ error: 'Failed to save encrypted
data.' });
  }
});
// Route to retrieve encrypted data
router.get('/secure-data/:fileName', async (req, res) => {
  const fileName = req.params.fileName;
  try {
    const decryptedData = await readEncryptedData(fileName);
    res.send(decryptedData);
```

```
  } catch (err) {
    res.status(500).json({ error: 'Failed to retrieve
encrypted data.' });
  }
});
module.exports = router;
```

Then, integrating data routes into the server

```
// file: app.js
const dataRoutes = require('./routes/dataRoutes');
// ... other imports
app.use('/api', dataRoutes);
// ... other routes
// Start the server
// ... server setup
```

And, finally testing encrypted data storage and retrieval.

- Save Encrypted Data:

```
curl -k -X POST -H "Content-Type: application/json" -d
'{"fileName":"confidential.txt","data":"This is highly
sensitive information."}' https://localhost:3000/api/secure-
data/save
```

- Retrieve Encrypted Data:

```
curl -k https://localhost:3000/api/secure-
data/confidential.txt
```

By integrating the **crypto** module into our book publishing platform, we've established robust mechanisms for securing sensitive data. We've implemented password hashing to protect user credentials, encryption and decryption of manuscripts and other sensitive files, secure token generation for authentication processes, and digital signatures to ensure data integrity. Additionally, we've utilized secure random number generation for creating tokens and implemented key exchange protocols to establish secure communication channels. These practices collectively enhance the security posture of our application, safeguarding both user data and the platform's integrity.

Summary

Throughout Chapter 5, we delved deeply into the intricacies of managing file systems and data streams within a Node.js environment. We began by mastering advanced file system operations, learning how to perform asynchronous tasks, monitor file changes, and manage file permissions effectively. This foundational knowledge enabled us to handle user-uploaded files, organize directories systematically, and ensure that sensitive data remained secure through appropriate permission settings.

Moving forward, we explored the power of streams for efficient data processing. By understanding readable, writable, duplex, and transform streams, we optimized our application to handle large volumes of data without overwhelming system memory. This was particularly beneficial when dealing with extensive manuscripts or multimedia content, as streams allowed us to process data incrementally and maintain high performance. We also ventured into creating custom stream implementations, which provided tailored solutions for specific data processing needs, such as real-time text analysis and secure data transformations.

Managing large data sets with buffers was another critical aspect we tackled. Buffers allowed us to handle binary data efficiently, enabling tasks like image processing and binary file manipulation without significant memory overhead. By implementing buffer-based techniques, we ensured that our application remained responsive and scalable, even when processing substantial amounts of data. Additionally, we learned to prevent memory leaks and optimize buffer usage, which further enhanced the application's stability and performance.

The chapter concluded with an in-depth integration of the crypto module to secure sensitive data. We implemented hashing for password protection, employed cipher algorithms for encrypting and decrypting manuscripts, and utilized secure random number generation for creating robust tokens. These cryptographic practices fortified our application's security, safeguarding user information and maintaining data integrity across various operations. Overall, Chapter 5 equipped us with the essential tools and techniques to manage file systems and data streams proficiently, ensuring our book publishing platform was both efficient and secure.

Knowledge Exercise

1. Which Node.js module provides the primary methods for interacting with the file system?

A. path

B. fs

C. stream

D. crypto

2. What is the primary advantage of using asynchronous file operations in Node.js?

A. They are easier to implement than synchronous operations.

B. They prevent blocking the event loop, enhancing performance.

C. They consume less memory compared to synchronous operations.

D. They automatically handle file permissions.

3. Which method from the fs module is used to watch for changes in a file or directory?

A. fs.watchFile()

B. fs.monitor()

C. fs.observe()

D. fs.watch()

4. In the context of file permissions, what does the mode 0o600 signify?

A. Read and write permissions for the owner, and no permissions for others.

B. Read, write, and execute permissions for everyone.

C. Read permissions for the owner and group, write for others.

D. Execute permissions for the owner only.

5. Which type of stream in Node.js is capable of both reading and writing data?

A. Readable

B. Writable

C. Duplex

D. Transform

6. What is the purpose of the _transform method in a custom Transform stream?

A. To initialize the stream's internal state.

B. To handle the transformation of each chunk of data passing through the stream.

C. To finalize the stream after all data has been processed.

D. To manage error handling within the stream.

7. How does a Buffer in Node.js differ from a standard JavaScript string?

A. Buffers are immutable, while strings are mutable.

B. Buffers are designed for binary data, whereas strings are for UTF-8 encoded text.

C. Buffers can only store numeric data, while strings store characters.

D. Buffers automatically manage memory, unlike strings.

8. Which crypto module method is suitable for securely generating random bytes for tokens?

A. crypto.randomFill()

B. crypto.randomBytes()

C. crypto.secureRandom()

D. crypto.generateRandom()

9. What is the primary purpose of hashing passwords before storing them?

A. To compress the password data for efficient storage.

B. To convert passwords into a fixed-size representation, enhancing security.

C. To encrypt passwords so they can be decrypted when needed.

D. To format passwords according to system requirements.

10. Which cipher algorithm was used in the practical examples for encrypting data?

A. DES

B. AES-256-CBC

C. RSA

D. Blowfish

11. What does the pipe() method do when working with streams in Node.js?

A. It closes the stream after use.

B. It transfers data from a readable stream to a writable stream automatically.

C. It transforms the data passing through the stream.

D. It pauses the stream until data processing is complete.

12. In the context of streams, what is backpressure?

A. When a stream receives more data than it can process at a time, causing it to slow down or pause.

B. When data flows in the opposite direction of the intended stream flow.

C. When a stream duplicates data to multiple destinations.

D. When a stream automatically resumes after an error occurs.

13. Which method is used to create a custom readable stream in Node.js?

A. Extending the **Readable** class and implementing the **_read** method.

B. Using the **fs.createReadStream()** function.

C. Implementing the **_write** method in the **Writable** class.

D. Combining **fs.watch()** with event listeners.

14. What is the role of an Initialization Vector (IV) in encryption algorithms like AES?

A. To generate the encryption key from a password.

B. To provide randomness, ensuring that identical plaintexts encrypt to different ciphertexts.

C. To compress the data before encryption.

D. To store the encrypted data securely.

15. How does the crypto.pbkdf2 function enhance password security?

A. By encrypting the password so it can be decrypted later.

B. By generating a unique salt and applying multiple hashing iterations to make brute-force attacks more difficult.

C. By converting the password into a binary format.

D. By storing the password in plain text with additional metadata.

Answers and Explanations

1. B. fs

The **fs** module in Node.js provides the primary methods for interacting with the file system, including reading, writing, and watching files and directories.

2. B. They prevent blocking the event loop, enhancing performance.

Asynchronous file operations allow Node.js to handle other tasks while waiting for file operations to complete, preventing the event loop from being blocked and thus improving application performance.

3. D. fs.watch()

The **fs.watch()** method is used to monitor changes in a file or directory, emitting events when modifications occur.

4. A. Read and write permissions for the owner, and no permissions for others.

The mode 0o600 sets read and write permissions for the file owner and removes all permissions for group and others, enhancing security.

5. C. Duplex

Duplex streams are capable of both reading and writing data, allowing data to flow in both directions.

6. B. To handle the transformation of each chunk of data passing through the stream.

The **_transform** method in a custom Transform stream processes each chunk of data, allowing for modification or transformation before passing it along.

7. B. Buffers are designed for binary data, whereas strings are for UTF-8 encoded text.

Buffers are used to handle binary data efficiently, while standard JavaScript strings are intended for UTF-8 encoded text.

8. B. crypto.randomBytes()

The **crypto.randomBytes()** method securely generates random bytes, suitable for creating tokens and other cryptographic purposes.

9. B. To convert passwords into a fixed-size representation, enhancing security.

Hashing passwords transforms them into a fixed-size string, making it difficult to reverse-engineer the original password and enhancing security.

10. B. AES-256-CBC

AES-256-CBC was used in the practical examples for encrypting and decrypting data, providing strong symmetric encryption.

11. B. It transfers data from a readable stream to a writable stream automatically.

The **pipe()** method connects a readable stream to a writable stream, facilitating the automatic flow of data between them.

12. A. When a stream receives more data than it can process at a time, causing it to slow down or pause.

Backpressure occurs when a writable stream cannot process incoming data as quickly as a readable stream provides it, necessitating flow control mechanisms.

13. A. Extending the Readable class and implementing the _read method.

To create a custom readable stream, one typically extends the **Readable** class and implements the _read method to define how data is supplied to the stream.

14. B. To provide randomness, ensuring that identical plaintexts encrypt to different ciphertexts.

An Initialization Vector (IV) introduces randomness into the encryption process, ensuring that the same plaintext encrypts differently each time, enhancing security.

15. B. By generating a unique salt and applying multiple hashing iterations to make brute-force attacks more difficult.

The **crypto.pbkdf2** function derives a cryptographic key from a password using a unique salt and numerous iterations, significantly increasing the effort required for brute-force attacks.

CHAPTER 6: ADVANCED APIS AND UTILITY MODULES

Overview

In this chapter, we'll take a look at some of the more advanced APIs and utility modules that can really make Node.js applications more functional and robust. We'll start by looking at how to create command line interfaces (CLIs) with the help of the Readline module, which allows you to make user-friendly and interactive CLI tools.

We also look at the nitty-gritty of parsing and handling URLs and query strings. The key to getting the most out of your data is knowing how to break down and work with the different parts of a URL. This helps you capture the right information and use it in the best way, which improves performance and user experience. The chapter also looks at how to find and fix errors using the Domain and V8 modules. By using these modules, we learned how to create isolated environments that prevent crashes across the whole application, which makes our systems more stable and reliable. We also looked at data compression with the Zlib module, which gave us the tools to make data storage and transmission more efficient.

Finally, we'll look at how to integrate external APIs and services. This lets us extend our applications' capabilities by using third-party functionalities. This integration makes it easier to add features like payment processing, data analytics, and social media interactions. This broadens the scope and utility of our Node.js projects. Overall, this chapter provides a great step-by-step guide to using advanced Node.js modules and APIs. This helps us build more sophisticated, efficient, and resilient applications.

Developing CLIs with Readline

The Readline module provides an interface for reading data from a Readable stream (such as **process.stdin**) one line at a time. It facilitates the creation of interactive prompts, command parsing, and real-time user input handling, making it indispensable for CLI development. Whether you're building a simple interactive prompt or a complex command interpreter, Readline offers the necessary tools to manage user interactions seamlessly.

We will begin by setting up a basic Readline interface, guiding you through initializing the module and handling simple user inputs. As we progress, we'll explore more advanced functionalities, such as implementing command history, autocompletion, and handling special key presses. By the end of this section, you'll be equipped to design and develop interactive command-line applications that respond dynamically to user inputs, enhancing both usability and functionality.

To illustrate the practical application of Readline, we'll develop a sample CLI tool that manages a simple to-do list, in which we learn to prompt users for input, process commands, and provide real-time feedback.

Readline Module Overview

The Readline module in Node.js is designed to facilitate the creation of interactive command-line applications. It allows developers to read user input from the terminal, process commands, and provide immediate feedback. The module handles the complexities of input buffering, line editing, and event management, enabling you to focus on implementing the core functionalities of your CLI tool.

Key Features of the Readline Module:

- Reads input one line at a time, ideal for processing commands.
- Displays customizable prompts to guide user interactions.
- Emits events for various input actions, such as **`line`**, **`close`**, and **`SIGINT`**.
- Maintains a history of entered commands for easy navigation.
- Supports autocompletion of commands and inputs to enhance user experience.

The Readline module is the ideal choice for developing sophisticated CLI applications. Its features streamline the development process, ensuring smooth and efficient user interactions.

Setting up Readline Interface

I'm going to show you how to create a simple CLI application that prompts the user for their name and greets them. This is a fundamental example that will teach you how to initialize the Readline interface and handle user input. Let's get started.

Initializing Readline Interface

First, we'll require the Readline module and create an interface connected to the standard input (**process.stdin**) and standard output (**process.stdout**).

```
// file: cli.js
const readline = require('readline');
// Create Readline Interface
const rl = readline.createInterface({
  input: process.stdin,
  output: process.stdout,
  prompt: 'Enter your name: '
});
```

In the above script,

- **`readline.createInterface`** initializes a new Readline interface.
- **`Input`** specifies the input stream, typically **`process.stdin`**.
- **`Output`** specifies the output stream, typically **`process.stdout`**. And,
- **`Prompt`** sets the initial prompt displayed to the user.

Displaying Prompt and Handling Input

Now here, we'll display the prompt and set up an event listener to handle the user's input.

```
// Display the prompt
rl.prompt();
// Event listener for 'line' event
rl.on('line', (line) => {
  const name = line.trim();
  console.log(`Hello, ${name}!`);
  rl.close();
}).on('close', () => {
  console.log('Goodbye!');
  process.exit(0);
});
```

In the above script,

- **`rl.prompt()`** displays the prompt to the user.
- **`rl.on('line', callback)`** listens for the 'line' event, which is triggered when the user presses Enter.
- **`line.trim()`** removes any leading/trailing whitespace from the input.
- **`rl.close()`** closes the Readline interface, triggering the 'close' event.
- **`rl.on('close', callback)`** handles the closure of the interface, allowing for graceful termination of the application.

Save the **cli.js** file and then execute it.

This simple application demonstrates how to initialize the Readline interface, display prompts, handle user input, and terminate the application gracefully.

Implement Command Handling

We're going to take the basic interface and build a more interactive CLI tool that can handle multiple commands, including adding tasks to a to-do list, viewing tasks, and exiting the application.

Designing CLI Structure

We'll design a CLI with the following commands:

- **add <task>**: Adds a new task to the to-do list.
- **view**: Displays all current tasks.
- **exit**: Exits the application.

Setting up To-Do List Data Structure

We'll use an array to store the tasks in memory.

```
// file: todoCLI.js
const readline = require('readline');
// Initialize Readline Interface
const rl = readline.createInterface({
  input: process.stdin,
  output: process.stdout,
  prompt: 'todo> '
});
// To-Do List Array
const todoList = [];
// Display the prompt
rl.prompt();
// Event Listener for 'line' Event
rl.on('line', (line) => {
  const input = line.trim();
  const [command, ...args] = input.split(' ');
  switch (command.toLowerCase()) {
    case 'add':
      addTask(args.join(' '));
      break;
    case 'view':
      viewTasks();
      break;
    case 'exit':
```

```
      rl.close();
      break;
    default:
      console.log(`Unknown command: ${command}`);
      break;
  }
  rl.prompt();
}).on('close', () => {
  console.log('Exiting To-Do CLI. Goodbye!');
  process.exit(0);
});
// Function to Add a Task
function addTask(task) {
  if (task) {
    todoList.push(task);
    console.log(`Added task: "${task}"`);
  } else {
    console.log('Error: No task provided. Usage: add <task>');
  }
}
// Function to View All Tasks
function viewTasks() {
  if (todoList.length === 0) {
    console.log('No tasks in the to-do list.');
  } else {
    console.log('To-Do List:');
    todoList.forEach((task, index) => {
      console.log(`${index + 1}. ${task}`);
    });
```

```
  }
}
```

Save the **todoCLI.js** file and execute it:

```
node todoCLI.js
```

Following can be a simple or a sample interaction:

```
todo> add Buy groceries
Added task: "Buy groceries"
todo> add Schedule meeting with team
Added task: "Schedule meeting with team"
todo> view
To-Do List:
1. Buy groceries
2. Schedule meeting with team
todo> exit
Exiting To-Do CLI. Goodbye!
```

This improved CLI application shows you how to handle multiple commands, manage a simple data structure, and provide real-time feedback to the user. You can create versatile and interactive command-line tools for various use cases by parsing commands and executing corresponding functions.

Enhancing CLI with Command History and Autocompletion

We must improve the user experience by adding command history navigation and autocompletion features to our CLI application. These enhancements will make the tool more intuitive and user-friendly.

Implementing Command History

The Readline module automatically maintains a history of entered commands, allowing users to navigate through previous inputs using the up and down arrow keys. However, to persist history across sessions, we need to implement a mechanism to save and load history from a file.

So to do this, we'll save the command history to a **.history** file each time the application exits.

```
const fs = require('fs');
const path = require('path');
const historyFile = path.join(__dirname, '.history');
// Load History from File
if (fs.existsSync(historyFile)) {
  const history = fs.readFileSync(historyFile,
'utf8').split('\n').reverse();
  rl.history.push(...history);
}
// Event Listener for 'close' Event to Save History
rl.on('close', () => {
  fs.writeFileSync(historyFile,
rl.history.slice().reverse().join('\n'), 'utf8');
  console.log('Exiting To-Do CLI. Goodbye!');
  process.exit(0);
});
```

Here,

- **`fs.existsSync(historyFile)`** checks if the history file exists.
- **`fs.readFileSync(historyFile, 'utf8').split('\n').reverse()`** reads and splits the history file into an array, reversing it to match Readline's history order.
- **`rl.history.push(...history);`** pushes the loaded history into the Readline interface.
- When the interface closes, **`rl.on('close', callback)`** writes the current history to the **`.history`** file.
- **`rl.history.slice().reverse().join('\n')`** reverses the history array to maintain chronological order before saving.

Adding Autocompletion

Autocompletion boosts efficiency by letting users complete commands with a single tab. We're implementing autocompletion for our predefined commands. **add**, **view**, and **exit**.

First, create an array of available commands to use for autocompletion.

```
const commands = ['add', 'view', 'exit'];
```

The completer function determines how autocompletion suggestions are generated based on user input.

```
// Completer Function
function completer(line) {
  const completions = commands;
  const hits = completions.filter((c) => c.startsWith(line));
  // Show all completions if none found
  return [hits.length ? hits : completions, line];
}
// Reinitialize Readline Interface with Completer
const rl = readline.createInterface({
  input: process.stdin,
  output: process.stdout,
  prompt: 'todo> ',
  completer: completer
});
```

Here, the **completer(line)** receives the current input line and filters the **commands** array to find matches that start with the entered text. And, the **return [hits.length ? hits : completions, line];** returns the matching completions or all commands if no matches are found.

And then finally, restart the CLI application and try typing partial commands followed by the Tab key.

Handling Special Key Presses and Interrupt Signals

Managing special key presses, such as **Ctrl+C** for interrupting the application, ensures that your CLI tool behaves predictably and allows users to exit gracefully.

The **SIGINT** signal is emitted when the user presses **Ctrl+C**. Handling this signal allows the application to perform cleanup tasks before exiting.

```
rl.on('SIGINT', () => {
  rl.question('Are you sure you want to exit? (y/n) ',
(answer) => {
```

```
    if (answer.match(/^y(es)?$/i)) rl.close();
    else rl.prompt();
  });
});
```

Here,

- rl.on('SIGINT', callback) listens for the SIGINT signal.
- **rl.question(prompt, callback)** asks the user for confirmation before exiting.
- **answer.match(/^y(es)?$/i)** checks if the user's response starts with 'y' or 'yes' (case-insensitive).

Then, run the CLI application and press **Ctrl+C** to trigger the interrupt signal.

Following is a sample interaction:

```
todo> ^C
Are you sure you want to exit? (y/n) n
todo>
```

If the user confirms, the application exits; otherwise, it continues running.

Incorporating Autocompletion for Task Numbers

To further enhance usability, we can implement autocompletion for task numbers when executing commands like **delete** and **complete**. This feature allows users to quickly select tasks without manually typing their numbers.

Modifying Completer Function

We'll update the completer function to provide context-sensitive suggestions based on the current command.

```
function completer(line) {
  const [command, ...args] = line.trim().split(' ');
  let completions = [];
  switch (command.toLowerCase()) {
    case 'add':
      completions = []; // No autocompletion for add command
```

```
      break;
    case 'delete':
    case 'complete':
      completions = todoList.map((_, index) => (index +
1).toString());
      break;
    case 'view':
    case 'save':
    case 'load':
    case 'exit':
      completions = commands.filter(c => c.startsWith(line));
      break;
    default:
      completions = commands.filter(c => c.startsWith(line));
      break;
  }
  const hits = completions.filter((c) => c.startsWith(args[0]
|| ''));
  return [hits.length ? hits : completions, args[0] || ''];
}
```

In the above script, the completer function examines the current command and provides relevant suggestions.

- For **delete** and **complete** commands, it suggests task numbers based on the current **todoList**.
- For other commands, it suggests the available command names.

Updating Readline Interface

Here, ensure that the Readline interface is updated with the new completer function.

```
const rl = readline.createInterface({
  input: process.stdin,
```

```
  output: process.stdout,
  prompt: 'todo> ',
  completer: completer
});
```

Testing Enhanced Autocompletion

To do thi, run the CLI application and test autocompletion for task numbers. Let us say following is the sample interaction:

```
todo> add Prepare for presentation
Added task: "Prepare for presentation"
todo> add Organize team meeting
Added task: "Organize team meeting"
todo> view
To-Do List:
1. [ ] Prepare for presentation
2. [ ] Organize team meeting
todo> delete <TAB>
1 2
todo> delete 1
Deleted task: "Prepare for presentation"
todo> view
To-Do List:
1. [ ] Organize team meeting
```

By pressing **<TAB>** after typing **delete**, the CLI suggests available task numbers, streamlining the command execution process.

Handling Input Validation and Error Messages

Robust CLI applications provide clear feedback and handle invalid inputs gracefully. We'll enhance our to-do list CLI by adding input validation and informative error messages.

Validating Command Inputs

It's important to make sure that the commands are given the right arguments and that those arguments are valid.

```
// Function to Add a Task
function addTask(task) {
  if (task) {
    todoList.push({ description: task, completed: false });
    console.log(`Added task: "${task}"`);
  } else {
    console.log('Error: No task provided. Usage: add <task>');
  }
}
// Function to Delete a Task
function deleteTask(taskNumber) {
  const index = parseInt(taskNumber, 10) - 1;
  if (isNaN(index) || index < 0 || index >= todoList.length) {
    console.log('Error: Invalid task number. Usage: delete
<task number>');
    return;
  }
  const removed = todoList.splice(index, 1);
  console.log(`Deleted task: "${removed[0].description}"`);
}
// Function to Complete a Task
function completeTask(taskNumber) {
  const index = parseInt(taskNumber, 10) - 1;
  if (isNaN(index) || index < 0 || index >= todoList.length) {
    console.log('Error: Invalid task number. Usage: complete
<task number>');
    return;
  }
```

```
  if (todoList[index].completed) {
    console.log(`Task "${todoList[index].description}" is
already completed.`);
    return;
  }
  todoList[index].completed = true;
  console.log(`Marked task "${todoList[index].description}" as
completed.`);
}
```

Providing Informative Error Messages

If something goes wrong, helpful error messages will show you what's wrong and what the app expects from you.

- Missing Arguments:

```
todo> add
Error: No task provided. Usage: add <task>
```

- Invalid Task Number:

```
todo> delete 5
Error: Invalid task number. Usage: delete <task number>
```

- Completing an Already Completed Task:

```
todo> complete 1
Task "Organize team meeting" is already completed.
```

Integrating External APIs and Services

While the Readline module is primarily used for handling user input within the terminal, integrating external APIs and services can extend the functionality of your CLI applications. For instance, you might want to fetch data from a web service, interact with databases, or perform network operations based on user commands.

Fetching Data from an External API

Let's enhance our to-do CLI by allowing users to fetch motivational quotes from an external API. This feature can provide inspirational messages upon adding new tasks.

- Installing required packages

We'll use the **axios** library to make HTTP requests to external APIs.

```
npm install axios
```

- Implementing the Quote Fetching Function

```
// file: todoCLI.js
const axios = require('axios');
// Function to Fetch a Random Motivational Quote
async function fetchQuote() {
  try {
    const response = await
axios.get('https://api.quotable.io/random');
    return response.data.content;
  } catch (error) {
    console.error('Error fetching quote:', error.message);
    return 'Stay motivated and keep pushing forward!';
  }
}
```

- Updating add task function to include quotes

```
async function addTask(task) {
  if (task) {
    const quote = await fetchQuote();
    todoList.push({ description: task, completed: false });
    console.log(`Added task: "${task}"`);
    console.log(`Motivational Quote: "${quote}"`);
  } else {
    console.log('Error: No task provided. Usage: add <task>');
```

```
    }
}
```

- Modifying the 'line' event listener to support async functions

Since the **addTask** function is now asynchronous, we need to handle it accordingly.

```
rl.on('line', async (line) => {
  const input = line.trim();
  const [command, ...args] = input.split(' ');
  switch (command.toLowerCase()) {
    case 'add':
      await addTask(args.join(' '));
      break;
    case 'view':
      viewTasks();
      break;
    case 'delete':
      deleteTask(args[0]);
      break;
    case 'complete':
      completeTask(args[0]);
      break;
    case 'save':
      saveTasks();
      break;
    case 'load':
      loadTasks();
      break;
    case 'help':
      displayHelp();
```

```
      break;
    case 'exit':
      rl.close();
      break;
    default:
      console.log(`Unknown command: ${command}`);
      console.log('Type "help" to see available commands.');
      break;
  }
  rl.prompt();
});
```

Testing Integration with External API

Next, run the enhanced CLI application and add a new task to see the motivational quote.

```
todo> add Complete Chapter 6
Added task: "Complete Chapter 6"
Motivational Quote: "Success is not final, failure is not
fatal: It is the courage to continue that counts."
todo> view
To-Do List:
1. [ ] Complete Chapter 6
todo> exit
Exiting To-Do CLI. Goodbye!
```

Here, the integration showcases how external APIs can enrich CLI applications by providing additional functionalities and enhancing user engagement.

Incorporating Error Isolation

Ensuring that errors within specific parts of your CLI application do not crash the entire application is crucial for maintaining stability. While the Readline module manages user interactions, integrating error isolation mechanisms can help contain and handle errors gracefully.

Understanding Domain and V8 Modules

The Domain module provides a way to handle multiple different IO operations as a single group. If any event emitter within a domain emits an error, the domain object can handle it, preventing the application from crashing.

And, the V8 module exposes information about the underlying V8 engine, such as heap statistics and memory usage, which can be useful for monitoring and debugging purposes.

Implementing Error Isolation with Domain Module

While the Domain module is deprecated in newer versions of Node.js, understanding its use can provide insights into error handling. Instead, modern applications often use try-catch blocks and error event listeners.

- Handling errors in command functions

Just make sure that each command function handles its own errors so that you don't end up with unhandled exceptions.

```
// Example: Safe Delete Function
function deleteTask(taskNumber) {
  try {
    const index = parseInt(taskNumber, 10) - 1;
    if (isNaN(index) || index < 0 || index >= todoList.length)
{
      throw new Error('Invalid task number.');
    }
    const removed = todoList.splice(index, 1);
    console.log(`Deleted task: "${removed[0].description}"`);
  } catch (error) {
    console.log(`Error: ${error.message} Usage: delete <task
number>`);
  }
}
```

- Wrapping asynchronous operations with error handlers

For asynchronous operations like saving and loading tasks, ensure that errors are caught and handled appropriately.

```
function saveTasks() {
  fs.writeFile(todoFilePath, JSON.stringify(todoList, null,
2), 'utf8', (err) => {
    if (err) {
      console.error(`Error saving tasks: ${err.message}`);
    } else {
      console.log('Tasks saved successfully.');
    }
  });
}
function loadTasks() {
  fs.readFile(todoFilePath, 'utf8', (err, data) => {
    if (err) {
      console.error(`Error loading tasks: ${err.message}`);
    } else {
      try {
        todoList = JSON.parse(data);
        console.log('Tasks loaded successfully.');
      } catch (parseErr) {
        console.error(`Error parsing tasks:
${parseErr.message}`);
      }
    }
  });
}
```

Monitoring Memory Usage with V8 Module

While not directly related to error isolation, monitoring memory usage can help detect potential issues that may lead to errors.

```
const v8 = require('v8');
```

```
// Function to Display Memory Usage
function displayMemoryUsage() {
  const heapStats = v8.getHeapStatistics();
  console.log('Memory Usage:');
  console.log(`  Total Heap Size: ${(heapStats.total_heap_size / 1024 / 1024).toFixed(2)} MB`);
  console.log(`  Used Heap Size: ${(heapStats.used_heap_size / 1024 / 1024).toFixed(2)} MB`);
  console.log(`  Heap Size Limit: ${(heapStats.heap_size_limit / 1024 / 1024).toFixed(2)} MB`);
}
// Periodically Display Memory Usage
setInterval(displayMemoryUsage, 60000); // Every 60 seconds
```

In the above script, **v8.getHeapStatistics()** retrieves statistics about the V8 engine's heap, including total heap size, used heap size, and heap size limit.

Data Compression with 'Zlib'

The Zlib module offers methods to compress and decompress data using algorithms like Gzip and Deflate. Integrating Zlib into your CLI application can reduce file sizes, speed up data transmission, and conserve storage space.

Compressing and Decompressing To-Do List

We'll enhance our to-do CLI by adding commands to compress and decompress the to-do list file (**todoList.json**). This feature allows users to save space and manage backups efficiently.

- Importing 'Zlib' module

```
const zlib = require('zlib');
```

- Implementing compress function

```
function compressTasks() {
  fs.readFile(todoFilePath, (err, data) => {
    if (err) {
      console.error(`Error reading tasks: ${err.message}`);
```

```
      return;
    }
    zlib.gzip(data, (err, buffer) => {
      if (err) {
        console.error(`Error compressing tasks:
${err.message}`);
        return;
      }
      const compressedFilePath = `${todoFilePath}.gz`;
      fs.writeFile(compressedFilePath, buffer, (err) => {
        if (err) {
          console.error(`Error saving compressed tasks:
${err.message}`);
        } else {
          console.log('Tasks compressed and saved
successfully.');
        }
      });
    });
  });
}
```

- Implementing the decompress function

```
function decompressTasks() {
  const compressedFilePath = `${todoFilePath}.gz`;
  fs.readFile(compressedFilePath, (err, buffer) => {
    if (err) {
      console.error(`Error reading compressed tasks:
${err.message}`);
      return;
    }
```

```
    zlib.gunzip(buffer, (err, data) => {
      if (err) {
        console.error(`Error decompressing tasks:
${err.message}`);
        return;
      }
      try {
        todoList = JSON.parse(data);
        console.log('Tasks decompressed and loaded
successfully.');
      } catch (parseErr) {
        console.error(`Error parsing tasks:
${parseErr.message}`);
      }
    });
  });
}
```

- Adding new commands to CLI

Here, update the **commands** array and the event listener to include the new **compress** and **decompress** commands.

```
const commands = ['add', 'view', 'delete', 'complete', 'save',
'load', 'compress', 'decompress', 'exit'];
// Function to Display Help
function displayHelp() {
  console.log('Available Commands:');
  console.log('  add <task>          - Add a new task');
  console.log('  view                - View all tasks');
  console.log('  delete <task #>     - Delete a task');
  console.log('  complete <task #> - Mark a task as
completed');
```

```
  console.log('  save                 - Save tasks to a file');
  console.log('  load                 - Load tasks from a file');
  console.log('  compress             - Compress the tasks
file');
  console.log('  decompress           - Decompress the tasks
file');
  console.log('  exit                 - Exit the application');
}
// Adding Command Handlers
rl.on('line', async (line) => {
  const input = line.trim();
  const [command, ...args] = input.split(' ');
  switch (command.toLowerCase()) {
    case 'add':
      await addTask(args.join(' '));
      break;
    case 'view':
      viewTasks();
      break;
    case 'delete':
      deleteTask(args[0]);
      break;
    case 'complete':
      completeTask(args[0]);
      break;
    case 'save':
      saveTasks();
      break;
    case 'load':
      loadTasks();
```

```
      break;
    case 'compress':
      compressTasks();
      break;
    case 'decompress':
      decompressTasks();
      break;
    case 'help':
      displayHelp();
      break;
    case 'exit':
      rl.close();
      break;
    default:
      console.log(`Unknown command: ${command}`);
      console.log('Type "help" to see available commands.');
      break;
  }
  rl.prompt();
});
```

Testing Data Compression and Decompression

Run the CLI application and execute the new commands.

```
todo> add Review Chapter 5
Added task: "Review Chapter 5"
Motivational Quote: "The only way to do great work is to love
what you do."
todo> add Test data compression
Added task: "Test data compression"
```

```
Motivational Quote: "Success usually comes to those who are
too busy to be looking for it."
todo> view
To-Do List:
1. [✓] Complete Chapter 6
2. [ ] Organize team meeting
3. [ ] Review Chapter 5
4. [ ] Test data compression
todo> save
Tasks saved successfully.
todo> compress
Tasks compressed and saved successfully.
todo> exit
Exiting To-Do CLI. Goodbye!
```

Upon restarting the application, use the **decompress** command to restore the to-do list from the compressed file.

```
todo> load
Tasks loaded successfully.
todo> view
To-Do List:
1. [✓] Complete Chapter 6
2. [ ] Organize team meeting
3. [ ] Review Chapter 5
4. [ ] Test data compression
todo> exit
Exiting To-Do CLI. Goodbye!
```

This demonstrates how the Zlib module can be integrated to manage data efficiently, reducing storage requirements and facilitating data portability. As you continue to expand your CLI applications, consider incorporating additional modules and services to further enhance functionality and user experience.

Parsing and Handling URLs and Query Strings

These days, web apps rely on URL and query string parsing to route users, retrieve data and provide a smooth experience. We'll look at how to work with URL parts in Node.js using built-in tools and practical techniques. If you know how URLs and query strings work, you can create dynamic routes, manage user inputs, and interact with external data sources more effectively. Once you've got a handle on these concepts, you can improve your application's routing logic, handle data better, and make sure the client and server interact in a reliable way.

Understanding URL Structure

Before we get started with parsing and handling URLs, we need to understand the different parts that make up a URL. A standard URL is made up of the following parts:

```
scheme://hostname:port/path?query#fragment
```

Here,

- **Scheme:** Specifies the protocol used (e.g., **`http`**, **`https`**, **`ftp`**).
- **Hostname:** The domain name or IP address of the server (e.g., **`www.example.com`**).
- **Port:** (Optional) The port number on which the server is listening (e.g., **`:80`** for HTTP).
- **Path:** The specific resource or endpoint on the server (e.g., **`/users/profile`**).
- **Query:** (Optional) Key-value pairs providing additional parameters (e.g., **`?id=123&sort=asc`**).
- **Fragment:** (Optional) An anchor within the resource (e.g., **`#section1`**).

If developers understand these components, they can parse URLs effectively, get the info they need, and construct URLs for various operations.

Parsing URLs

Node.js has the **URL** module, which is great for parsing and formatting URLs. It's not used as much as the WHATWG URL API, but it's still really useful for understanding URL parsing concepts.

- Using Legacy **`url`** Module

```
// file: urlParser.js
const url = require('url');
```

```
const myURL =
'https://www.example.com:8080/path/name?query=123&sort=asc#sec
tion1';
const parsedUrl = url.parse(myURL, true); // The second
parameter 'true' parses the query string into an object
console.log(parsedUrl);
```

Here, **url.parse(urlString, parseQueryString)** parses a URL string into an object. Setting **`parseQueryString`** to **`true`** converts the query string into an object.

Following is the output:

```
{
  protocol: 'https:',
  slashes: true,
  auth: null,
  host: 'www.example.com:8080',
  port: '8080',
  hostname: 'www.example.com',
  hash: '#section1',
  search: '?query=123&sort=asc',
  query: { query: '123', sort: 'asc' },
  pathname: '/path/name',
  path: '/path/name?query=123&sort=asc',
  href:
'https://www.example.com:8080/path/name?query=123&sort=asc#sec
tion1'
}
```

- Extracting URL Components

Using the parsed URL object, you can easily access different parts of the URL:

```
console.log(`Protocol: ${parsedUrl.protocol}`); // https:
console.log(`Hostname: ${parsedUrl.hostname}`); //
www.example.com
```

```
console.log(`Port: ${parsedUrl.port}`); // 8080
console.log(`Pathname: ${parsedUrl.pathname}`); // /path/name
console.log(`Query Parameters:`, parsedUrl.query); // { query:
'123', sort: 'asc' }
console.log(`Fragment: ${parsedUrl.hash}`); // #section1
```

Parsing URLs with 'WHATWG URL API'

The WHATWG URL API offers a more modern and standardized approach to URL parsing and manipulation as shown below:

```
// file: whatwgUrlParser.js
const { URL } = require('url');
const myURL = new
URL('https://www.example.com:8080/path/name?query=123&sort=asc
#section1');
console.log(myURL);
```

Here, **new URL(input[, base])** creates a new URL object. The **input** must be an absolute URL or relative to the **base**.

Handling Query Strings with 'querystring' Module

While the WHATWG URL API provides **URLSearchParams** for handling query parameters, the **querystring** module offers additional utilities for parsing and formatting query strings.

- Parsing Query Strings

```
// file: queryParser.js
const querystring = require('querystring');
const query = 'name=JohnDoe&age=30&city=NewYork';
const parsedQuery = querystring.parse(query);
console.log(parsedQuery);
```

Following is the output:

```
{
  name: 'JohnDoe',
```

```
  age: '30',
  city: 'NewYork'
}
```

- Stringifying Query Objects

```
const queryObj = {
  name: 'JaneDoe',
  age: '25',
  city: 'LosAngeles'
};
const queryString = querystring.stringify(queryObj);
console.log(queryString); //
name=JaneDoe&age=25&city=LosAngeles
```

- Integrating with URL Parsing

Combine **url** and **querystring** modules to parse full URLs and handle query parameters.

```
const url = require('url');
const querystring = require('querystring');
const myURL =
'https://www.example.com/search?term=nodejs&sort=desc';
const parsedUrl = url.parse(myURL);
const parsedQuery = querystring.parse(parsedUrl.query);
console.log(parsedQuery);
// Output: { term: 'nodejs', sort: 'desc' }
```

Constructing URLs for External API Integration

Sometimes, you have to create URLs with special query parameters to get data or send it. Let's look at a simple way of doing this based on what the user inputs or what the application is doing.

Fetching Data from an External API

Suppose we want to integrate a weather service API that provides current weather information based on city names.

- Defining the Base URL and API Key

```
const { URL } = require('url');
const WEATHER_API_BASE =
'https://api.openweathermap.org/data/2.5/weather';
const API_KEY = 'your_api_key_here'; // Replace with your
actual API key
```

- Building the URL with Query Parameters

```
function buildWeatherApiUrl(city) {
  const url = new URL(WEATHER_API_BASE);
  url.searchParams.append('q', city);
  url.searchParams.append('appid', API_KEY);
  url.searchParams.append('units', 'metric'); // For
temperature in Celsius
  return url.toString();
}
// Example Usage
const city = 'London';
const weatherUrl = buildWeatherApiUrl(city);
console.log(weatherUrl);
// Output:
https://api.openweathermap.org/data/2.5/weather?q=London&appid
=your_api_key_here&units=metric
```

Making HTTP Requests to External API

Using the **https** module or a library like **axios**, you can send requests to the constructed URL and handle the responses. See the following using **axios**:

```
const axios = require('axios');
async function getWeather(city) {
  const url = buildWeatherApiUrl(city);
  try {
```

```
    const response = await axios.get(url);
    const data = response.data;
    console.log(`Weather in ${data.name}:
${data.weather[0].description}, Temperature:
${data.main.temp}°C`);
  } catch (error) {
    console.error('Error fetching weather data:',
error.response ? error.response.data : error.message);
  }
}
// Example Usage
getWeather('New York');
```

Here,

- **`new URL(base)`** initializes a new URL object with the base URL.
- url.searchParams.append(key, value) adds query parameters to the URL.
- **`url.toString()`** converts the URL object back to a string for use in HTTP requests.
- **`axios.get(url)`** sends a GET request to the specified URL.

Handling Nested and Complex Query Parameters

Some applications require handling nested or complex query parameters, especially when dealing with structured data. So here, suppose you want to filter products based on multiple attributes like category, price range, and availability.

- Constructing the URL

```
http://localhost:3000/products/filter?category=electronics&pri
ce[min]=500&price[max]=1500&available=true
```

- Parsing Nested Query Parameters with `qs` Module

The **querystring** module in Node.js does not handle nested objects well. Instead, use the **qs** library.

```
npm install qs
// file: expressAppWithQs.js
const express = require('express');
```

```
const app = express();
const PORT = 3000;
const qs = require('qs');
// Sample Data
const products = [
  { id: 1, name: 'Laptop', category: 'electronics', price: 1200, available: true },
  { id: 2, name: 'Smartphone', category: 'electronics', price: 800, available: false },
  { id: 3, name: 'Desk Chair', category: 'furniture', price: 150, available: true },
  { id: 4, name: 'Book', category: 'literature', price: 20, available: true }
];
// Middleware to Parse Complex Query Strings
app.use((req, res, next) => {
  req.query = qs.parse(req.url.split('?')[1]);
  next();
});
// Filter Route
app.get('/products/filter', (req, res) => {
  const { category, price, available } = req.query;
  let filteredProducts = [...products];
  if (category) {
    filteredProducts = filteredProducts.filter(p => p.category === category);
  }
  if (price) {
    if (price.min) {
      filteredProducts = filteredProducts.filter(p => p.price >= parseFloat(price.min));
```

```
    }
    if (price.max) {
      filteredProducts = filteredProducts.filter(p => p.price
<= parseFloat(price.max));
    }
  }
  if (available !== undefined) {
    const isAvailable = available === 'true';
    filteredProducts = filteredProducts.filter(p =>
p.available === isAvailable);
  }
  res.json(filteredProducts);
});
// Start Server
app.listen(PORT, () => {
  console.log(`Express.js server is running at
http://localhost:${PORT}/`);
});
```

- Testing the Complex Filter Route

First, start the server:

```
node expressAppWithQs.js
```

Now, access the filter route:

```
http://localhost:3000/products/filter?category=electronics&pri
ce[min]=500&price[max]=1500&available=true
```

Following will be the response:

```
[
  { "id": 1, "name": "Laptop", "category": "electronics",
"price": 1200, "available": true }
```

```
]
```

In the above, the **qs** library parses nested query parameters into JavaScript objects, allowing for more straightforward data manipulation.

Redirecting and Rewriting URLs

Sometimes, it's necessary to redirect users to different URLs or rewrite incoming URLs to match specific routing patterns.

- Implementing redirects in Express.js

```
app.get('/old-route', (req, res) => {
  res.redirect(301, '/new-route'); // Permanent redirect
});
app.get('/new-route', (req, res) => {
  res.send('You have been redirected to the new route.');
});
```

- Rewriting URLs using Middleware

Middleware can intercept requests and modify the URL before it reaches the route handlers.

```
// Redirect all '/admin/*' routes to '/dashboard/*'
app.use('/admin', (req, res, next) => {
  req.url = req.url.replace('/admin', '/dashboard');
  next();
});
app.get('/dashboard/settings', (req, res) => {
  res.send('Admin Settings Page');
});
```

In this,

- Redirects tells clients to make new requests to different URLs. This is useful for removing old routes or changing how the application is structured.
- And, URL rewriting changes request URLs so they match different route handlers, without telling clients. This is good for keeping URLs clean or implementing proxy-like behaviors.

Handling URL Encoding and Decoding

It's important to encode and decode URLs correctly to make sure special characters are transmitted properly and securely.

- Encoding URL Components

```
const { encodeURIComponent } = require('querystring');
const city = 'New York';
const encodedCity = encodeURIComponent(city);
console.log(encodedCity); // New%20York
```

- Decoding URL Components

```
const { decodeURIComponent } = require('querystring');
const encodedCity = 'New%20York';
const decodedCity = decodeURIComponent(encodedCity);
console.log(decodedCity); // New York
```

For instance, here are the encoding parameters for API requests:

```
function buildSearchUrl(base, params) {
  const url = new URL(base);
  Object.keys(params).forEach(key => {
    url.searchParams.append(key, params[key]);
  });
  return url.toString();
}
const searchParams = {
  query: 'Node.js tutorials',
  page: 1
};
const searchUrl =
buildSearchUrl('https://www.example.com/search',
searchParams);
```

```
console.log(searchUrl);
// Output:
https://www.example.com/search?query=Node.js%20tutorials&page=
1
```

In this case, **encodeURIComponent** replaces certain characters in a URI with one, two, three, or four escape sequences. These represent the UTF-8 encoding of the character. And, **decodeURIComponent** reverses this process. It replaces each escape sequence in the encoded URI component with the character that it represents.

If you get to grips with these concepts and techniques, you can build solid, scalable, and secure Node.js applications that can handle all kinds of routing and data retrieval challenges. Being able to parse URLs and manage query strings is a great skill to have because it lets you create dynamic and user-centric web applications.

Summary

In a nutshell, we looked at some pretty advanced APIs and utility modules that gave our Node.js apps a major boost. We started off by taking a look at the Readline module to create some cool CLIs. We used Readline to create some pretty sophisticated CLI tools. They can handle real-time user input, manage command histories, and provide autocompletion. This makes our applications more user-friendly and efficient.

Next, we moved on to the tricky business of parsing and handling URLs and query strings. We learned how to break down URLs, get the query parameters, and make URLs that fit different apps by using both the old URL module and the new WHATWG URL API. The chapter also showed us how to find and fix errors by introducing us to the Domain and V8 modules. We put in place ways to spot and deal with errors in specific parts of our applications, which made our software more stable and reliable overall. On top of that, keeping an eye on memory usage with the V8 module helped us see how the application was performing and spot any memory leaks. Another big focus was data compression. We used the Zlib module to make data storage and transmission more efficient. By implementing compression and decompression techniques, we reduced bandwidth usage and improved the efficiency of our applications, especially when handling large datasets.

Last but not least, integrating external APIs and services expanded the functionality of our applications. We learned how to construct and manipulate URLs for making API requests, handle responses, and incorporate third-party functionalities such as fetching data from external sources.

Knowledge Exercise

1. Which Node.js module is primarily used to create interactive CLIs by reading input one line at a time?

A. process

B. readline

C. commander

D. inquirer

2. What method from the Readline module is used to display a prompt to the user?

A. rl.displayPrompt()

B. rl.showPrompt()

C. rl.prompt()

D. rl.writePrompt()

3. In the Readline module, which event is emitted whenever the user inputs a line and presses Enter?

A. input

B. data

C. line

D. end

4. Which built-in Node.js module provides utilities for parsing and formatting URLs?

A. path

B. querystring

C. url

D. http

5. What is the primary purpose of the URLSearchParams interface in Node.js?

A. To parse URL fragments

B. To handle HTTP headers

C. To work with query string parameters

D. To manage URL pathnames

6. Which Node.js module allows developers to handle binary data efficiently, often used alongside the zlib module for data compression?

A. buffer

B. stream

C. crypto

D. fs

7. What function from the zlib module is commonly used to compress data using the Gzip algorithm?

A. zlib.deflate()

B. zlib.gzip()

C. zlib.brotliCompress()

D. zlib.compress()

8. When integrating external APIs, which Node.js module is typically used to make HTTP requests?

A. fs

B. http

C. https

D. net

9. What is the primary role of the V8 module in Node.js applications?

A. To manage file system operations

B. To handle network requests

C. To expose information about the V8 JavaScript engine

D. To provide cryptographic functionalities

10. Which method from the readline module allows for implementing custom autocompletion in a CLI application?

A. rl.setCompleter()

B. rl.autocomplete()

C. rl.on('autocomplete')

D. rl.completer()

11. What is the purpose of using the domain module in Node.js applications?

A. To handle DNS resolutions

B. To manage application-wide configurations

C. To provide a way to handle multiple different I/O operations as a single group for error handling

D. To create secure domains for web hosting

12. Which zlib method would you use to decompress data that was compressed using the Deflate algorithm?

A. zlib.inflate()

B. zlib.unzip()

C. zlib.gunzip()

D. zlib.decompress()

13. When constructing URLs for external API requests, which component is essential for specifying the desired data format, such as JSON?

A. Protocol

B. Hostname

C. Pathname

D. Query Parameters

14. Which event should be listened to in the Readline interface to gracefully handle the termination of a CLI application when the user presses Ctrl+C?

A. exit

B. SIGTERM

C. close

D. SIGINT

15. In the context of integrating external APIs, what is the primary advantage of using asynchronous HTTP requests in Node.js?

A. They are easier to debug than synchronous requests

B. They prevent blocking the event loop, allowing the application to handle other tasks concurrently

C. They automatically retry failed requests

D. They ensure data is always received in order

Answers and Explanations

1. B. readline

The readline module in Node.js is specifically designed to create interactive CLIs by reading input from a readable stream (like process.stdin) one line at a time.

2. C. rl.prompt()

The rl.prompt() method from the Readline module displays the configured prompt to the user, indicating that the application is ready to receive input.

3. C. line

The line event is emitted by the Readline interface whenever the user inputs a line and presses Enter. This event is essential for processing user commands or inputs.

4. C. url

The url module provides utilities for URL resolution and parsing, allowing developers to dissect and manipulate various components of a URL.

5. C. To work with query string parameters

URLSearchParams is an interface that provides methods to work with the query string of a URL, enabling easy retrieval, addition, and modification of query parameters.

6. B. stream

The stream module allows handling of streaming data in Node.js, which is essential for efficiently processing large amounts of binary data, especially when combined with modules like zlib for compression.

7. B. zlib.gzip()

The zlib.gzip() method compresses data using the Gzip algorithm, which is widely used for reducing the size of data before storage or transmission.

8. C. https

While both http and https modules can be used to make HTTP requests, the https module is typically preferred for making secure requests to external APIs that require encryption.

9. C. To expose information about the V8 JavaScript engine

The V8 module provides access to information and statistics about the V8 engine, such as memory usage and heap statistics, which can be useful for performance monitoring and debugging.

10. A. rl.setCompleter()

The rl.setCompleter() method allows developers to define a custom completer function for implementing autocompletion in CLI applications, enhancing user experience by suggesting possible command completions.

11. C. To provide a way to handle multiple different I/O operations as a single group for error handling

The domain module was designed to simplify error handling by grouping multiple I/O operations and handling errors collectively. However, it's deprecated in newer Node.js versions in favor of other error-handling patterns.

12. A. zlib.inflate()

The zlib.inflate() method decompresses data that was compressed using the Deflate algorithm, reversing the compression process to retrieve the original data.

13. D. Query Parameters

When constructing URLs for external API requests, query parameters are essential for specifying data formats, such as requesting a response in JSON by including parameters like format=json.

14. D. SIGINT

The SIGINT signal is emitted when the user presses Ctrl+C. Listening to this event allows the application to handle termination gracefully, such as by performing cleanup tasks before exiting.

15. B. They prevent blocking the event loop, allowing the application to handle other tasks concurrently

Asynchronous HTTP requests enable Node.js applications to remain responsive by not blocking the event loop while waiting for external API responses. This concurrency allows the application to handle other operations simultaneously, improving overall performance and efficiency.

CHAPTER 7: PERFORMANCE OPTIMIZATION AND TESTING

Overview

In this last chapter, we're going to look at the most important parts of making Node.js apps run faster and test them better. We'll start by looking at profiling and monitoring techniques, which help us spot performance problems and get real-time insights into how our applications are working. Next, we'll look at how to manage and collect garbage in your Node.js apps to keep them stable and prevent leaks. We'll learn how to keep an eye on how much memory our applications are using and make sure they stay responsive and strong even when they're under a lot of pressure. Then, we'll move on to writing comprehensive unit and integration tests using popular frameworks like Mocha and Jest. We'll also look at how to structure tests, mock dependencies, and automate testing processes to make our development workflow more efficient.

Finally, we'll explore the implementation of continuous integration and deployment (CI/CD) pipelines. We'll learn how to integrate various tools and services to create a seamless CI/CD pipeline that supports rapid and reliable application deployments. All in all, this chapter will equip us with the knowledge and skills to build high-performance, well-tested, and efficiently deployed Node.js applications.

Profiling and Monitoring Node.js Applications

Ensuring that your Node.js applications perform optimally is crucial, especially as they grow in complexity and user base. Profiling and monitoring are essential practices that help identify performance bottlenecks, memory leaks, and inefficient resource usage. In this section, we will explore practical techniques using Node.js's inbuilt tools to profile and monitor our ongoing sample application—a comprehensive command-line to-do list tool. By the end of this guide, you will be equipped to analyze your application's performance, pinpoint areas for improvement, and implement optimizations to enhance efficiency and responsiveness.

We will begin by utilizing the Node.js Inspector, an inbuilt profiling tool that integrates seamlessly with Chrome DevTools.

Setting up Node.js Inspector

The Node.js Inspector is an inbuilt tool that allows you to debug and profile your application using Chrome DevTools. It provides a comprehensive interface for monitoring CPU and memory usage, setting breakpoints, and inspecting variables.

Starting the Inspector

To begin profiling, you need to start your Node.js application with the **--inspect** flag. This flag enables the Inspector and opens a debugging port.

```
node --inspect todoCLI.js
```

Upon running this command, you will see an output similar to:

```
Debugger listening on ws://127.0.0.1:9229/abcd1234...
For help see https://nodejs.org/en/docs/inspector
```

Connecting Chrome DevTools

- Launch Google Chrome on your machine. Navigate to **chrome://inspect** in the address bar.
- Under the "Remote Target" section, you should see your running Node.js application listed. Click the "inspect" link next to your application to open Chrome DevTools connected to your Node.js process.

Profiling CPU Usage

The good thing about profiling CPU usage is that it helps you identify which functions or processes are using too much processing power, which can lead to slow application performance.

- In Chrome DevTools, go to the "Profiler" tab. Click the "Start" button to begin recording a CPU profile.
- Perform actions in your to-do CLI that you suspect may be causing performance issues, such as adding multiple tasks or performing complex searches.
- After completing the interactions, click the "Stop" button to end the recording. The profiler will display a flame chart illustrating the call stack and the time spent in each function. Look for functions with the highest CPU usage.

Suppose you notice that adding tasks takes longer as the list grows. By profiling, you might discover that the **addTask** function has a quadratic time complexity due to inefficient data handling.

```
function addTask(input) {
  if (input) {
    const parts = input.split('|').map(part => part.trim());
    const description = parts[0] || 'No Description';
    const priorityMatch = parts[1] ?
parts[1].match(/Priority:\s*(\w+)/i) : null;
    const dueDateMatch = parts[2] ? parts[2].match(/Due
Date:\s*(\d{4}-\d{2}-\d{2})/i) : null;
    const priority = priorityMatch ? priorityMatch[1] : 'Low';
```

```
    const dueDate = dueDateMatch ? dueDateMatch[1] : '2024-12-
31';
    // Inefficient push operation
    todoList.push({
      id: todoList.length + 1,
      description,
      priority,
      dueDate,
      completed: false
    });
    console.log(`Added task: "${description}" - Priority:
${priority} - Due: ${dueDate}`);
  } else {
    console.log('Error: No task provided. Usage: add <task> |
Priority: <priority> | Due Date: <YYYY-MM-DD>');
  }
}
```

The profiler highlights that as **todoList** grows, the **push** operation becomes more time-consuming, indicating a need for optimization.

Monitoring Memory Usage

If your app is leaking memory, it can end up using more and more memory over time, which can cause it to crash or slow down. Keeping an eye on how much memory your app is using can help you catch these issues early.

Using process.memoryUsage()

The **process.memoryUsage()** method returns an object detailing the memory usage of the Node.js process.

```
function logMemoryUsage() {
  const memory = process.memoryUsage();
  console.log('Memory Usage:');
```

```
  console.log(`  RSS: ${(memory.rss / 1024 / 1024).toFixed(2)}
MB`);
  console.log(`  Heap Total: ${(memory.heapTotal / 1024 /
1024).toFixed(2)} MB`);
  console.log(`  Heap Used: ${(memory.heapUsed / 1024 /
1024).toFixed(2)} MB`);
  console.log(`  External: ${(memory.external / 1024 /
1024).toFixed(2)} MB`);
}
// Example Usage
setInterval(logMemoryUsage, 60000); // Logs memory usage every
60 seconds
```

Analyzing Heap Snapshots

Heap snapshots provide a detailed view of memory allocation within your application. To capture a heap snapshot:

- In Chrome DevTools, navigate to the "Memory" tab. Click on "Take Heap Snapshot" to capture the current state of memory usage.
- Examine the allocation of objects, identifying any unexpected growth or retention of objects that should have been garbage collected.

Suppose repeated additions of tasks without proper deletion cause memory usage to spike. By taking heap snapshots before and after adding tasks, you can compare the number and size of objects to identify leaks.

Implementing Continuous Monitoring

For ongoing performance assessment, integrating continuous monitoring tools ensures that any degradation in performance is promptly detected and addressed.

Using Built-in Monitoring Tools

Node.js provides several methods for continuous monitoring:

- **`process.cpuUsage()`** returns the user and system CPU time used by the current process.

`process.memoryUsage()` provides detailed memory usage statistics.

For instance, we've got a real-time monitoring script as below:

```
function monitorPerformance() {
  const cpu = process.cpuUsage();
  const memory = process.memoryUsage();
  console.log('CPU Usage:');
  console.log(`  User: ${(cpu.user / 1000).toFixed(2)} ms`);
  console.log(`  System: ${(cpu.system / 1000).toFixed(2)}
ms`);

  console.log('Memory Usage:');
  console.log(`  RSS: ${(memory.rss / 1024 / 1024).toFixed(2)}
MB`);
  console.log(`  Heap Total: ${(memory.heapTotal / 1024 /
1024).toFixed(2)} MB`);
  console.log(`  Heap Used: ${(memory.heapUsed / 1024 /
1024).toFixed(2)} MB`);
  console.log(`  External: ${(memory.external / 1024 /
1024).toFixed(2)} MB`);

  console.log('----------------------------------------');
}
// Monitor every 30 seconds
setInterval(monitorPerformance, 30000);
```

This script logs CPU and memory usage at regular intervals, providing continuous insights into the application's performance.

Optimizing Identified Bottlenecks

Once profiling and monitoring reveal performance issues, the next step is to optimize the code to eliminate these bottlenecks.

Refactoring Inefficient Functions

Continuing with our earlier example, suppose the **addTask** function becomes inefficient as the task list grows. To optimize, we can implement more efficient data structures or algorithms.

Following is the original **addTask** function:

```
function addTask(input) {
  if (input) {
    const parts = input.split('|').map(part => part.trim());
    const description = parts[0] || 'No Description';
    const priorityMatch = parts[1] ?
parts[1].match(/Priority:\s*(\w+)/i) : null;
    const dueDateMatch = parts[2] ? parts[2].match(/Due
Date:\s*(\d{4}-\d{2}-\d{2})/i) : null;
    const priority = priorityMatch ? priorityMatch[1] : 'Low';
    const dueDate = dueDateMatch ? dueDateMatch[1] : '2024-12-
31';
    todoList.push({
      id: todoList.length + 1,
      description,
      priority,
      dueDate,
      completed: false
    });
    console.log(`Added task: "${description}" - Priority:
${priority} - Due: ${dueDate}`);
  } else {
    console.log('Error: No task provided. Usage: add <task> |
Priority: <priority> | Due Date: <YYYY-MM-DD>');
  }
}
```

Given below is the optimized **addTask** function:

```
function addTask(input) {
  if (!input) {
```

```
    console.log('Error: No task provided. Usage: add <task> |
Priority: <priority> | Due Date: <YYYY-MM-DD>');
    return;
  }
  const parts = input.split('|').map(part => part.trim());
  const description = parts[0] || 'No Description';
  const priority = (parts[1] &&
parts[1].match(/Priority:\s*(\w+)/i)) ?
parts[1].match(/Priority:\s*(\w+)/i)[1] : 'Low';
  const dueDate = (parts[2] && parts[2].match(/Due
Date:\s*(\d{4}-\d{2}-\d{2})/i)) ? parts[2].match(/Due
Date:\s*(\d{4}-\d{2}-\d{2})/i)[1] : '2024-12-31';
  // Using a unique ID generator instead of relying on array
length
  const id = generateUniqueId();
  todoList.push({
    id,
    description,
    priority,
    dueDate,
    completed: false
  });
  console.log(`Added task: "${description}" - Priority:
${priority} - Due: ${dueDate}`);
}
// Function to generate unique IDs
const { v4: uuidv4 } = require('uuid');
function generateUniqueId() {
  return uuidv4();
}
```

Reducing Memory Footprint

Suppose the application retains unnecessary references to completed tasks, preventing garbage collection and increasing memory usage. To address this, we can implement task pruning.

```
function pruneCompletedTasks() {
  const beforePrune = todoList.length;
  todoList = todoList.filter(task => !task.completed);
  const afterPrune = todoList.length;
  console.log(`Pruned ${beforePrune - afterPrune} completed
tasks.`);
}
// Example Usage
setInterval(pruneCompletedTasks, 3600000); // Prunes every
hour
```

By periodically removing completed tasks, we reduce the memory footprint and maintain optimal performance.

Automating Performance Monitoring

If you automate your performance monitoring, you can assess continuously without any manual input.

- Using **`perf_hooks`** for Custom Metrics

```
const { PerformanceObserver, performance } =
require('perf_hooks');
// Create an observer instance
const obs = new PerformanceObserver((list) => {
  const entry = list.getEntries()[0];
  console.log(`${entry.name}: ${entry.duration} ms`);
  performance.clearMarks();
});
obs.observe({ entryTypes: ['measure'] });
// Example: Measuring Execution Time
```

```
function addTask(input) {
  performance.mark('start-addTask');
  if (input) {
    const parts = input.split('|').map(part => part.trim());
    const description = parts[0] || 'No Description';
    const priorityMatch = parts[1] ?
parts[1].match(/Priority:\s*(\w+)/i) : null;
    const dueDateMatch = parts[2] ? parts[2].match(/Due
Date:\s*(\d{4}-\d{2}-\d{2})/i) : null;
    const priority = priorityMatch ? priorityMatch[1] : 'Low';
    const dueDate = dueDateMatch ? dueDateMatch[1] : '2024-12-
31';
    const id = generateUniqueId();
    todoList.push({
      id,
      description,
      priority,
      dueDate,
      completed: false
    });
    console.log(`Added task: "${description}" - Priority:
${priority} - Due: ${dueDate}`);
  } else {
    console.log('Error: No task provided. Usage: add <task> |
Priority: <priority> | Due Date: <YYYY-MM-DD>');
  }
  performance.mark('end-addTask');
  performance.measure('addTask Execution Time', 'start-
addTask', 'end-addTask');
}
```

Here in the above script,

- `performance.mark()` creates markers at specific points in the code.
- `performance.measure()` calculates the duration between two marks.

PerformanceObserver listens for performance measurements and logs them, providing insights into function execution times.

Through hands-on profiling and optimization, we have not only improved the current performance issues but also established a robust foundation for ongoing performance management. This proactive approach to performance optimization and monitoring is essential for developing high-quality Node.js applications that meet the demands of real-world usage.

Memory Management and Garbage Collection Techniques

Making sure we're managing memory effectively is really important for keeping Node.js apps running smoothly and reliably. In this section, we'll take a look at how Node.js handles memory through the V8 JavaScript engine. We'll take a look at some key metrics and tools that help us keep an eye on memory usage, spot potential issues, and understand memory usage patterns better. Next, we'll look at ways to make the most of the memory we have in our to-do list app. This means making changes to the code to use memory more efficiently, managing data structures wisely, and getting rid of any unnecessary references to make garbage collection easier. We'll also go over the best ways to handle large datasets, asynchronous operations, and event listeners to make sure we don't accidentally keep memory around.

Finally, we'll look at ways to spot and stop memory leaks, which are when memory that's no longer needed isn't released back to the system. We'll use Node.js's built-in tools, like heap snapshots and memory profiling, to find the usual places where our application leaks memory. Then we'll put in place fixes to stop these leaks, so our to-do list tool stays strong and fast even when it's used a lot. This way of looking after memory will help you build Node.js apps that work well for a long time without slowing down.

Understanding Node.js Memory Management

Node.js depends on the V8 JavaScript engine, which takes care of memory allocation and garbage collection for you. As software developers, it's important to understand how V8 manages memory to write efficient, leak-free code.

Memory Allocation

When your application creates objects, arrays, or other data structures, V8 allocates memory for them.

There are two primary memory regions:

- **Heap Memory:** Used for dynamic memory allocation where objects are stored.
- **Stack Memory:** Used for static memory allocation, such as function calls and primitive data types.

Garbage Collection (GC)

Garbage collection is the process by which V8 automatically frees memory that is no longer in use. It identifies objects that are no longer reachable from the root (global objects) and reclaims their memory. Understanding how GC works helps in writing code that minimizes memory overhead and prevents leaks.

Following are the key memory metrics:

- **RSS (Resident Set Size):** Total memory allocated for the process, including heap, stack, and C++ objects.
- **Heap Total:** Total size of the allocated heap.
- **Heap Used:** Actual memory used by the application within the heap.
- **External:** Memory used by C++ objects bound to JavaScript objects managed by V8.

Keeping an eye on these metrics gives you a good idea of how your application is using memory.

Monitoring Memory Usage in To-Do List App

To keep our to-do list application running smoothly, we need to keep an eye on how it's using memory over time. Node.js has lots of built-in tools and methods that make this easy.

Using process.memoryUsage()

The **process.memoryUsage()** method returns an object detailing the current memory usage of the Node.js process.

```
function logMemoryUsage() {
  const memory = process.memoryUsage();
  console.log('Memory Usage:');
  console.log(`  RSS: ${(memory.rss / 1024 / 1024).toFixed(2)} MB`);
  console.log(`  Heap Total: ${(memory.heapTotal / 1024 / 1024).toFixed(2)} MB`);
  console.log(`  Heap Used: ${(memory.heapUsed / 1024 / 1024).toFixed(2)} MB`);
  console.log(`  External: ${(memory.external / 1024 / 1024).toFixed(2)} MB`);
```

```
}
// Example Usage
setInterval(logMemoryUsage, 60000); // Logs memory usage every
60 seconds
```

Heap Snapshots with Chrome DevTools

Heap snapshots provide a detailed view of memory allocation, allowing you to identify objects that persist in memory longer than necessary.

- Start the Inspector:

```
node --inspect todoCLI.js
```

- Open Chrome DevTools. Navigate to **`chrome://inspect`** in Google Chrome and click "inspect" next to your Node.js application.
- Capture a Heap Snapshot by visiting to the "Memory" tab. Click "Take Heap Snapshot". And then analyze the retained objects and identify potential leaks.

Optimizing Memory Usage

Optimizing memory usage involves writing efficient code, choosing appropriate data structures, and ensuring that memory is released when no longer needed.

Avoiding Unnecessary References

Make sure you de-reference objects when you're done with them so that the garbage collector can free up their memory.

```
function deleteTask(taskId) {
  const index = todoList.findIndex(task => task.id ===
taskId);
  if (index !== -1) {
    todoList.splice(index, 1);
    console.log(`Deleted task with ID: ${taskId}`);
  } else {
    console.log(`Task with ID: ${taskId} not found.`);
  }
}
```

In the above function, removing a task from **todoList** eliminates references to that task, allowing GC to reclaim its memory.

Managing Event Listeners

Excessive or improperly managed event listeners can lead to memory leaks. Ensure that listeners are removed when no longer needed.

```
const EventEmitter = require('events');
const emitter = new EventEmitter();
function onTaskAdded(task) {
  console.log(`Task added: ${task.description}`);
}
emitter.on('add', onTaskAdded);
// Later, to prevent memory leaks
emitter.removeListener('add', onTaskAdded);
```

Limiting Heap Size

Node.js allows you to set the maximum heap size using the **--max-old-space-size** flag. Adjusting this can help manage memory usage, especially for large applications.

```
node --max-old-space-size=2048 todoCLI.js
```

This command sets the maximum heap size to 2GB.

Preventing Memory Leaks

When memory that's no longer needed isn't released, it can cause a memory leak, which means the memory usage increases over time. It's really important to identify and prevent leaks to keep the application stable.

Common Sources of Memory Leaks

If you accidentally create global variables, it can stop the garbage collector from doing its job.

```
// Avoid
function addTask(input) {
  global.newTask = { description: input, completed: false };
```

```
}
```

Instead, use local variables or module-scoped variables.

Another thing closures can do is keep a link to variables from the outer scope.

```
function createAdder() {
  const largeArray = new Array(1000000).fill('leak');
  return function add(num) {
    return num + 1;
  };
}
const adder = createAdder();
```

In this example, **largeArray** remains in memory because the closure retains a reference to it.

Leveraging Garbage Collection

The more you understand how V8's garbage collector works, the better you can code to make the most of your memory.

Generational Garbage Collection

V8 employs a generational garbage collection strategy, categorizing objects into:

- **Young Generation:** Short-lived objects. Efficiently collected using Scavenge.
- **Old Generation:** Long-lived objects. Collected using Mark-Sweep and Mark-Compact.

Avoiding Long-Lived Object References

It's good practice to release references quickly to avoid unnecessary objects in the "Old Generation."

```
function processTasks() {
  let largeData = generateLargeDataSet();

  // Process data
  // ...
  // Release reference
```

```
  largeData = null;
}
```

Here, setting variables to **null** allows V8 to reclaim memory during the next garbage collection cycle.

Using Performance Hooks

The **perf_hooks** module provides APIs to measure performance metrics, offering deeper insights into memory usage and execution times.

```
const { PerformanceObserver, performance } =
require('perf_hooks');
function addTask(input) {
  performance.mark('start-addTask');

  // Task addition logic
  // ...
  performance.mark('end-addTask');
  performance.measure('addTask', 'start-addTask', 'end-
addTask');
}
const obs = new PerformanceObserver((list) => {
  const entry = list.getEntriesByName('addTask')[0];
  console.log(`addTask executed in
${entry.duration.toFixed(2)} ms`);
});
obs.observe({ entryTypes: ['measure'] });
```

What's in it for you?

- You can track the time taken for specific functions to complete.
- You can also use it to identify and optimise functions that are running slowly.

By integrating these memory management practices into our development workflow, we ensure that our Node.js applications remain performant, scalable, and resilient against memory-related issues. Mastery of these techniques is essential for building robust applications capable of handling increasing workloads without compromising on efficiency or user experience.

Writing Unit and Integration Tests with Mocha and Jest

Testing is a fundamental aspect of software development that ensures your application behaves as expected, maintains reliability, and facilitates future enhancements. In this section, we will guide you through setting up two of the most popular testing frameworks in the Node.js ecosystem: Mocha and Jest. We will then apply these frameworks to write both unit and integration tests for our ongoing sample application—the comprehensive command-line to-do list tool. By the end of this guide, you will be proficient in implementing effective testing strategies that enhance the quality and robustness of your Node.js applications.

Setting up Mocha and Jest

Before writing tests, we need to set up Mocha and Jest in our project. This involves installing the necessary packages and configuring our project to recognize and execute these tests.

Installing Mocha and Jest

Install Mocha and Jest as development dependencies:

```
npm install --save-dev mocha jest
```

Installing Assertion Libraries

While Jest comes with its own assertion library, Mocha does not. For Mocha, we can use Chai, a popular assertion library:

```
npm install --save-dev chai
```

Configuring Test Scripts

Update the **package.json** to include scripts for running tests with Mocha and Jest:

```
{
  "scripts": {
    "test:mocha": "mocha",
    "test:jest": "jest",
    "test": "npm run test:mocha && npm run test:jest"
```

```
  }
}
```

This configuration allows you to run Mocha tests with **npm run test:mocha**, Jest tests with **npm run test:jest**, and both sequentially with **npm test**.

Project Structure

Organize your project to separate source code from tests. A common structure is:

```
.
├── src
│   └── todoCLI.js
├── test
│   ├── mocha
│   │   └── todoCLI.test.js
│   └── jest
│       └── todoCLI.test.js
├── package.json
└── ...
```

Create a **test** directory with subdirectories for Mocha and Jest tests.

Writing Unit Tests with Mocha and Chai

Unit tests focus on individual components or functions, ensuring they work correctly in isolation. Let's write unit tests for some of the core functions in our to-do CLI application.

Assuming our **todoCLI.js** has the following functions:

```
// src/todoCLI.js
let todoList = [];
function addTask(description, priority = 'Low', dueDate =
'2024-12-31') {
  const task = {
    id: generateUniqueId(),
    description,
```

```
    priority,
    dueDate,
    completed: false
  };
  todoList.push(task);
  return task;
}
function deleteTask(id) {
  const index = todoList.findIndex(task => task.id === id);
  if (index !== -1) {
    return todoList.splice(index, 1)[0];
  }
  return null;
}
function completeTask(id) {
  const task = todoList.find(task => task.id === id);
  if (task) {
    task.completed = true;
    return task;
  }
  return null;
}
function getTasks() {
  return todoList;
}
function generateUniqueId() {
  return '_' + Math.random().toString(36).substr(2, 9);
}
module.exports = {
```

```
  addTask,
  deleteTask,
  completeTask,
  getTasks,
  generateUniqueId
};
```

Writing Mocha Unit Tests

Here, at first create a test file for Mocha: **test/mocha/todoCLI.test.js**.

```
// test/mocha/todoCLI.test.js
const { expect } = require('chai');
const {
  addTask,
  deleteTask,
  completeTask,
  getTasks,
  generateUniqueId
} = require('../../src/todoCLI');
describe('To-Do CLI Application - Mocha Unit Tests', () => {

  beforeEach(() => {
    // Reset todoList before each test
    while (getTasks().length > 0) {
      getTasks().pop();
    }
  });
  describe('addTask()', () => {
    it('should add a new task to the todoList', () => {
      const task = addTask('Test Task');
```

```
      expect(getTasks()).to.have.lengthOf(1);
      expect(getTasks()[0]).to.include({
        description: 'Test Task',
        priority: 'Low',
        dueDate: '2024-12-31',
        completed: false
      });
      expect(task).to.have.property('id');
    });
    it('should add a task with specified priority and
dueDate', () => {
      const task = addTask('Urgent Task', 'High', '2024-11-
30');
      expect(getTasks()).to.have.lengthOf(1);
      expect(getTasks()[0]).to.include({
        description: 'Urgent Task',
        priority: 'High',
        dueDate: '2024-11-30',
        completed: false
      });
    });
  });
  describe('deleteTask()', () => {
    it('should delete a task by id', () => {
      const task = addTask('Task to Delete');
      const deleted = deleteTask(task.id);
      expect(deleted).to.deep.equal(task);
      expect(getTasks()).to.have.lengthOf(0);
    });
```

```
    it('should return null when deleting a non-existent task',
() => {
      const deleted = deleteTask('nonexistentid');
      expect(deleted).to.be.null;
      expect(getTasks()).to.have.lengthOf(0);
    });
  });
  describe('completeTask()', () => {
    it('should mark a task as completed', () => {
      const task = addTask('Incomplete Task');
      const completedTask = completeTask(task.id);
      expect(completedTask).to.include({ completed: true });
      expect(getTasks()[0].completed).to.be.true;
    });
    it('should return null when completing a non-existent
task', () => {
      const completedTask = completeTask('nonexistentid');
      expect(completedTask).to.be.null;
    });
  });
  describe('generateUniqueId()', () => {
    it('should generate a unique ID', () => {
      const id1 = generateUniqueId();
      const id2 = generateUniqueId();
      expect(id1).to.be.a('string');
      expect(id2).to.be.a('string');
      expect(id1).to.not.equal(id2);
    });
  });
```

```
});
```

Running Mocha Tests

Then execute the Mocha tests using:

```
npm run test:mocha
```

You should see output indicating that all tests have passed, similar to:

```
To-Do CLI Application - Mocha Unit Tests
    addTask()
   ✓ should add a new task to the todoList
   ✓ should add a task with specified priority and dueDate
    deleteTask()
   ✓ should delete a task by id
   ✓ should return null when deleting a non-existent task
    completeTask()
   ✓ should mark a task as completed
   ✓ should return null when completing a non-existent task
    generateUniqueId()
   ✓ should generate a unique ID
  7 passing (XXms)
```

Writing Integration Tests with Jest

Integration tests check how different parts of your app work together, making sure they play nicely with each other. Jest is a handy testing framework that makes it easy to write and run integration tests.

Writing Jest Integration Tests

First, create a test file for Jest: **test/jest/todoCLI.test.js**.

```
// test/jest/todoCLI.test.js
const {
```

```
  addTask,
  deleteTask,
  completeTask,
  getTasks,
  generateUniqueId
} = require('../../src/todoCLI');
describe('To-Do CLI Application - Jest Integration Tests', ()
=> {
  beforeEach(() => {
    // Reset todoList before each test
    while (getTasks().length > 0) {
      getTasks().pop();
    }
  });
  test('Adding multiple tasks and retrieving them', () => {
    addTask('Task One');
    addTask('Task Two', 'Medium', '2024-11-15');
    addTask('Task Three', 'High', '2024-10-20');
    const tasks = getTasks();
    expect(tasks).toHaveLength(3);
    expect(tasks[0]).toMatchObject({
      description: 'Task One',
      priority: 'Low',
      dueDate: '2024-12-31',
      completed: false
    });
    expect(tasks[1]).toMatchObject({
      description: 'Task Two',
      priority: 'Medium',
```

```
      dueDate: '2024-11-15',
      completed: false
    });
    expect(tasks[2]).toMatchObject({
      description: 'Task Three',
      priority: 'High',
      dueDate: '2024-10-20',
      completed: false
    });
  });
  test('Completing a task and verifying its status', () => {
    const task = addTask('Incomplete Task');
    completeTask(task.id);
    const completedTask = getTasks().find(t => t.id ===
task.id);
    expect(completedTask.completed).toBe(true);
  });
  test('Deleting a task and ensuring it is removed', () => {
    const task1 = addTask('Task to Delete 1');
    const task2 = addTask('Task to Delete 2');
    deleteTask(task1.id);
    const tasks = getTasks();
    expect(tasks).toHaveLength(1);
    expect(tasks[0].id).toBe(task2.id);
  });
  test('Handling deletion of non-existent tasks gracefully',
() => {
    const result = deleteTask('nonexistentid');
    expect(result).toBeNull();
    expect(getTasks()).toHaveLength(0);
```

```
  });
  test('Ensuring unique IDs are generated for each task', ()
=> {
    const ids = new Set();
    for (let i = 0; i < 100; i++) {
      const id = generateUniqueId();
      expect(ids.has(id)).toBe(false);
      ids.add(id);
    }
  });
});
```

Running Jest Tests

And then execute the Jest tests using:

```
npm run test:jest
```

Here, Jest will provide a comprehensive report of the test results:

```
PASS  test/jest/todoCLI.test.js
  To-Do CLI Application - Jest Integration Tests
    ✓ Adding multiple tasks and retrieving them (XXms)
    ✓ Completing a task and verifying its status (XXms)
    ✓ Deleting a task and ensuring it is removed (XXms)
    ✓ Handling deletion of non-existent tasks gracefully
(XXms)
    ✓ Ensuring unique IDs are generated for each task (XXms)
Test Suites: 1 passed, 1 total
Tests:       5 passed, 5 total
Snapshots:   0 total
Time:        X.Xs
```

Integrating Tests into Development Workflow

I'd suggest you start incorporating testing into your daily development practices. That way, you'll be able to catch any issues early on and make sure the code is of a consistently high quality.

Continuous Testing

Run tests frequently during development to verify that new changes do not break existing functionality.

```
npm run test
```

This command executes both Mocha and Jest tests, providing a comprehensive test suite.

Test Automation with Pre-commit Hooks

Tools like Husky are great for automatically running tests before commits. This helps make sure that any faulty code doesn't make it into the codebase.

- Install Husky:

```
npm install --save-dev husky
```

- Initialize Husky:

```
npx husky install
```

- Add a Pre-commit Hook:

```
npx husky add .husky/pre-commit "npm run test"
```

This setup ensures that tests run before every commit, maintaining code integrity.

By setting up Mocha and Jest, and writing comprehensive unit and integration tests for our to-do CLI application, we have established a robust testing framework that ensures our application functions correctly and remains reliable as it evolves.

Implementing Continuous Integration and Deployment Pipelines

Continuous Integration (CI) and Continuous Deployment (CD) are key practices in modern software development. They help teams deliver high-quality apps quickly and reliably. In this section, we'll set up CI/CD pipelines for our ongoing sample application. We'll use GitHub Actions, a powerful and integrated CI/CD tool within GitHub, to automate testing, building, and deploying our application. By the end of this guide, you'll have a streamlined pipeline that ensures your application is consistently tested and deployed with each update.

GitHub Actions provides a seamless way to automate workflows directly within your GitHub repository. It allows you to define custom workflows that can be triggered by various events, such as code pushes, pull requests, or scheduled intervals. For our to-do CLI application, we will configure GitHub Actions to automatically run tests and deploy the application whenever changes are made to the main branch. This automation ensures that only tested and validated code is deployed, reducing the risk of introducing bugs into production.

Setting up CI Pipeline

The CI pipeline focuses on automatically building and testing your application whenever changes are pushed to the repository. Here's how to set it up using GitHub Actions:

Creating a Workflow File

In your repository on GitHub, click on the "Actions" tab. GitHub may suggest some workflow templates, but we will create a custom one.

Click on "Set up a workflow yourself" to create a new workflow file.

And then, name the workflow file **`ci-cd.yml`** and place it in the **`.github/workflows/`** directory.

Here's a sample configuration:

```
# .github/workflows/ci-cd.yml
name: CI/CD Pipeline
on:
  push:
    branches: [ main ]
  pull_request:
    branches: [ main ]
jobs:
  build-and-test:
    runs-on: ubuntu-latest
    steps:
      - name: Checkout Repository
        uses: actions/checkout@v3
```

```
      - name: Setup Node.js
        uses: actions/setup-node@v3
        with:
          node-version: '14'
          cache: 'npm'
      - name: Install Dependencies
        run: npm install
      - name: Run Mocha Tests
        run: npm run test:mocha
      - name: Run Jest Tests
        run: npm run test:jest
      - name: Build Application
        run: npm run build
  deploy:
    needs: build-and-test
    runs-on: ubuntu-latest
    if: github.ref == 'refs/heads/main' && github.event_name
== 'push'
    steps:
      - name: Checkout Repository
        uses: actions/checkout@v3
      - name: Setup Node.js
        uses: actions/setup-node@v3
        with:
          node-version: '14'
          registry-url: 'https://registry.npmjs.org/'
      - name: Install Dependencies
        run: npm install
      - name: Build Application
```

```
        run: npm run build
      - name: Publish to npm
        run: npm publish
        env:
          NODE_AUTH_TOKEN: ${{ secrets.NPM_TOKEN }}
```

Here, the workflow triggers on pushes and pull requests to the **main** branch.

The build-and-test job checks out the code, sets up Node.js, installs dependencies, runs Mocha and Jest tests, and builds the application.

And, the deploy job depends on the successful completion of build-and-test. It runs only on pushes to the main branch and handles deploying the application by publishing it to npm.

Configuring npm Publishing

Ensure your **`package.json`** includes necessary fields for publishing, such as **`name`**, **`version`**, **`main`**, and **`scripts`**. Add a **`build`** script if not already present.

```
{
  "name": "todo-cli-app",
  "version": "1.0.0",
  "main": "src/todoCLI.js",
  "scripts": {
    "test:mocha": "mocha",
    "test:jest": "jest",
    "build": "echo 'Building application...'"
  },
  "dependencies": {
    "uuid": "^8.3.2"
  },
  "devDependencies": {
    "chai": "^4.3.4",
    "mocha": "^9.1.3",
    "jest": "^27.3.1",
```

```
    "sinon": "^11.1.2"
  }
}
```

- To get an npm token, just log in to your npm account, go to "Access Tokens" in your profile settings, and generate a new automation token.
- Next, add the npm token to GitHub Secrets. To get to the "Settings" page on GitHub, just click on your profile picture in the top-right and then click on "Settings". From there, click on "Secrets and variables". You'll see a page with "Actions".
- Now, click "New repository secret" and name it NPM_TOKEN. And paste the generated npm token and save it.

Setting up CD Pipeline

The CD pipeline automates the deployment process, ensuring that tested code is deployed to production or made available to users seamlessly.

Publishing to npm

Publishing your CLI application to npm allows users to install it globally using **npm install -g todo-cli-app**. The **deploy** job in our workflow handles this.

Creating a Build Script

If your application requires a build step (e.g., transpiling with Babel), define it in your **package.json**. For simplicity, our sample application uses a placeholder build script.

```
"scripts": {
  "build": "echo 'Building application...'"
}
```

Replace this with actual build commands as needed.

Streamlining Delivery with CI/CD Pipeline

With the CI/CD pipeline configured, every push to the **main** branch triggers the workflow:

You can modify or add features to your to-do CLI application. For example, you could add a new command or improve existing functionality.

```
git add .
git commit -m "Add feature to prioritize tasks"
```

```
git push origin main
```

Navigate to the "Actions" tab in your GitHub repository. You will see the **CI/CD Pipeline** workflow running. Click on the workflow run to view detailed logs of each step—checking out code, installing dependencies, running tests, building, and deploying.

If all steps pass, your application is published to npm. You can verify by checking your npm package or attempting to install it globally.

If any step in the workflow fails (e.g., a test fails), GitHub Actions will mark the workflow as failed. You can inspect the logs to identify and fix the issue. Once resolved, commit the fixes and push again to trigger the pipeline.

Summary

This chapter gave us a thorough grasp on how to optimize and ensure the reliability of our Node.js to-do list application. We started by mastering Node.js's built-in profiling and monitoring tools, including the Inspector and perf_hooks. We analyzed CPU profiles and heap snapshots and identified inefficient code segments, then implemented optimisations that significantly improved our application's responsiveness and efficiency.

We learned handling memory allocation and garbage collection through the V8 engine, including how it manages memory. We used methods like **process.memoryUsage()** to monitor our application's memory consumption and identified and fixed potential memory leaks by examining heap snapshots. Furthermore, the chapter provided clear instructions on setting up and writing tests—unit and integration—using Mocha, Chai, and Jest. Finally, we implemented continuous integration and deployment pipelines using GitHub Actions. This automation ensured that every code change was thoroughly tested before being deployed, maintaining high code quality and reducing the risk of introducing errors into production.

This chapter equipped us with essential tools and practices for enhancing performance, managing memory efficiently, ensuring code reliability through testing, and automating deployment processes. These are critical for building scalable and maintainable Node.js applications.

Knowledge Exercise

1. Which Node.js module provides APIs for measuring performance metrics such as execution time and event loop delays?

A. process

B. perf_hooks

C. events

D. util

2. What command-line flag enables the Node.js Inspector for profiling and debugging applications?

A. --debug

B. --inspect

C. --profile

D. --monitor

3. Which method from the **process** module returns information about the memory usage of the Node.js process?

A. process.memoryInfo()

B. process.getMemoryUsage()

C. process.memoryUsage()

D. process.getHeapUsage()

4. In the context of garbage collection in Node.js, what does the term "heap snapshot" refer to?

A. A real-time graph of memory usage

B. A complete list of all objects in memory at a specific point in time

C. A summary of CPU usage

D. A log of garbage collection events

5. Which tool integrates with Node.js to provide a visual interface for profiling applications using Chrome DevTools?

A. PM2

B. Nodemon

C. Node Inspector

D. Forever

6. What is the primary difference between unit tests and integration tests?

A. Unit tests are written in JavaScript, while integration tests use other languages

B. Unit tests focus on individual components, whereas integration tests assess the interactions between components

C. Unit tests are automated, while integration tests are manual

D. There is no difference; the terms are interchangeable

7. Which assertion library is commonly used alongside Mocha for writing expressive tests?

A. Chai

B. Jest

C. Sinon

D. QUnit

8. What is the purpose of mocking in the context of unit testing?

A. To simulate user interactions

B. To replicate the entire application environment

C. To replace real dependencies with controlled stand-ins

D. To measure the performance of test cases

9. Which Jest feature allows developers to run tests related to files that have changed since the last commit?

A. Snapshot Testing

B. Watch Mode

C. Coverage Analysis

D. Test Sequencing

10. In GitHub Actions, what is the primary purpose of a workflow file typically located in **.github/workflows/?**

A. To store application configuration settings

B. To define automated tasks such as building, testing, and deploying code

C. To manage user permissions and access controls

D. To document the project's API endpoints

11. Which of the following is NOT a typical stage in a CI/CD pipeline?

A. Code Compilation

B. Automated Testing

C. Manual Code Review

D. Deployment

12. What environment variable is commonly used to securely store tokens or secrets required for deployment in CI/CD pipelines?

A. API_KEY

B. SECRET_TOKEN

C. ENV_VAR

D. NPM_TOKEN

13. How does PM2 assist in managing Node.js applications within a CI/CD pipeline?

A. By providing a graphical user interface for code editing

B. By automating database migrations

C. By managing application processes and offering built-in monitoring

D. By handling version control operations

14. Which GitHub Actions feature allows workflows to run jobs in parallel, reducing the total execution time?

A. Matrix Builds

B. Step Conditions

C. Caching

D. Artifact Uploads

15. What is the benefit of integrating automated testing into a CI/CD pipeline?

A. It eliminates the need for manual testing

B. It ensures that tests are only run when deploying to production

C. It automatically fixes bugs detected during testing

D. It verifies that new code changes do not break existing functionality before deployment

---

Answers and Explanations

1. B. perf_hooks

The **perf_hooks** module in Node.js provides APIs for measuring performance metrics, such as execution time of functions and event loop delays. It allows developers to create performance measurements and analyze the application's performance characteristics.

2. B. --inspect

The **--inspect** flag enables the Node.js Inspector, allowing developers to debug and profile applications using debugging tools like Chrome DevTools. This flag opens a debugging port, facilitating real-time profiling and debugging.

3. C. process.memoryUsage()

The **process.memoryUsage()** method returns an object containing information about the memory usage of the Node.js process, including properties like **rss**, **heapTotal**, **heapUsed**, and **external**.

4. B. A complete list of all objects in memory at a specific point in time

A heap snapshot is a detailed record of the memory allocation in an application at a particular moment. It lists all objects in memory, their types, and references, aiding in the identification of memory leaks and inefficient memory usage.

5. C. Node Inspector

Node Inspector is a tool that integrates with Node.js to provide a visual interface for profiling and debugging applications using Chrome DevTools. It allows developers to set breakpoints, inspect variables, and analyze performance metrics.

6. B. Unit tests focus on individual components, whereas integration tests assess the interactions between components

Unit tests are designed to test individual functions or modules in isolation to ensure they work correctly on their own. Integration tests, on the other hand, evaluate how different parts of the application interact with each other, ensuring that combined components function as intended.

7. A. Chai

Chai is a popular assertion library used alongside Mocha to write expressive and readable tests. It provides a variety of assertion styles, such as **expect**, **should**, and **assert**, enabling developers to articulate test conditions clearly.

8. C. To replace real dependencies with controlled stand-ins

Mocking involves creating fake versions of external dependencies or modules that mimic their behavior. This allows unit tests to run in isolation without relying on actual implementations, ensuring that tests are deterministic and focused on the component under test.

9. B. Watch Mode

Jest's Watch Mode monitors changes in the codebase and automatically runs tests related to the files that have been modified since the last commit. This feature provides immediate feedback during development, enhancing productivity.

10. B. To define automated tasks such as building, testing, and deploying code

A workflow file in **.github/workflows/** defines automated processes that GitHub Actions executes in response to specific events, such as code pushes or pull requests. These workflows can include tasks like running tests, building the application, and deploying it to production environments.

11. C. Manual Code Review

Typical stages in a CI/CD pipeline include code compilation, automated testing, and deployment. Manual code review, while important in the development process, is not considered a stage within the automated CI/CD pipeline itself.

12. D. NPM_TOKEN

Environment variables like **NPM_TOKEN** are used to securely store tokens or secrets required for deployment processes, such as publishing packages to npm. These tokens are kept in secure storage (e.g., GitHub Secrets) and accessed by CI/CD pipelines during deployment.

13. C. By managing application processes and offering built-in monitoring

PM2 is a process manager for Node.js applications that helps manage and keep applications running smoothly. It offers built-in monitoring, automatic restarts, and load balancing, which are beneficial within CI/CD pipelines for maintaining application uptime and performance.

14. A. Matrix Builds

Matrix Builds in GitHub Actions allow workflows to run multiple jobs in parallel based on defined parameters. This feature reduces the total execution time by executing different job configurations simultaneously.

15. D. It verifies that new code changes do not break existing functionality before deployment

Integrating automated testing into a CI/CD pipeline ensures that every code change is rigorously tested before being deployed. This process helps catch regressions and bugs early, maintaining the application's reliability and quality as it evolves.

Epilogue

I'm thrilled to be reaching the end of "JSNAD Certification Preparation" and looking back on the amazing journey we've had together! From the foundational concepts of Node.js to the intricate details of deployment and performance optimization, we've covered it all! Our exploration has been thorough and intensive, and I'm excited to share it with you. I've set out to create something really special: a resource that not only prepares you for the JSNAD exam, but also empowers you with the skills and confidence to excel in real-world Node.js development.

We've been breaking down complex topics throughout this book, and it's been a blast! We've been taking these complex topics and breaking them down into manageable sections that build upon each other. Each and every chapter was designed to reinforce your understanding and application of key Node.js principles, whether it was mastering asynchronous programming, implementing robust middleware, or setting up continuous integration pipelines. We've also included quick reference guides and a glossary of advanced terms to help you revise quickly and really understand challenging concepts. One of the most rewarding aspects of this journey has been the integration of sample projects and code repositories! These projects were an amazing way to put your new skills to the test! They gave you the chance to turn all that theoretical knowledge you'd gained into real, working code. I really hope you feel a sense of accomplishment and readiness as you complete this book! The JSNAD certification is a huge accomplishment that proves you're an expert in Node.js development and shows your dedication to the field.

You're all set to conquer the exam with the knowledge and strategies you've gained here! Remember that certification is not just about passing an exam; it's about solidifying your skills and positioning yourself for continued growth and success in the field. Looking ahead, I'm delighted to encourage you to build on the fantastic foundation you've already laid! Get involved with the Node.js community, contribute to open-source projects, and make sure you're up to date with the latest advancements! These steps will take your expertise to the next level and keep you at the cutting edge of development innovation. Ultimately, "JSNAD Certification Preparation" is so much more than just a study guide! It's a fantastic stepping stone towards greater professional achievement! I'm sure the insights and knowledge you've gained here will serve you well, both in the certification process and in your ongoing development career!

Thank You

www.ingramcontent.com/pod-product-compliance
Lightning Source LLC
Chambersburg PA
CBHW080210170726
48282CB00030B/1057
* 9 7 8 8 1 1 9 1 7 7 9 5 0 *